Britain & Ireland: Lives Entwined II

Essays on contemporary British–Irish relations, with views from the USA

BRITISH COUNCIL
Ireland

Acknowledgements

Thanks go to all who have worked on and contributed to *Britain & Ireland: Lives Entwined II*, in particular:

Rosemary Bechler for commissioning, organising and editing the essays that make up the book

Anne Sweetmore for proofreading and copy-editing services

Louise Leffler for typesetting services

Andrzej Krause, political cartoonist, for his illustrations

Abigail Davis and Jane Frewer at River Path Associates for design services

Victoria Collis at River Path Associates for editing services

Purely Print for printing the book

Contents

Preface: Mary McAleese, President of Ireland   4

Introduction: Tony Reilly, Director, British Council Ireland   6

A personal perspective on Ireland's relationship   12
with Britain: John Bruton

The American Connection: Kevin Cullen   34

Hyphenated hybrids: Irishness, Englishness and religious   48
identities in Britain and Ireland: Marianne Elliott

The peace process and journalism: Ed Moloney   64

The Hybrid Generation: Ivana Bacik   84

Colonial chains, domestic links: John A. Murphy   98

Lives Entangled: Bernadette McAliskey   118

Not for the faint-hearted: reflections on the Good Friday   132
Agreement, 8 years on: Liz O'Donnell

Red, white and blue – and true green too: taking new stock   150
of the American Irish: Ray O'Hanlon

The Outsider: Ruth Dudley Edwards   164

Rapparee Rap: Paul Muldoon   180

Preface
UACHTARÁN NA hÉIREANN
PRESIDENT OF IRELAND
Message from President McAleese

The spirit of real friendship and partnership that characterises the relationship between our two countries today is an inspiring example of what can be salvaged from the ashes of historical enmity and inequality.

The bond that exists between Ireland and the UK remains an extremely complex one, significantly defined by our intricately entwined histories and cultures. Yet, at the same time as it is important for us to recognise our shared past, present, and the future, it is a cause for great joy that both countries are now also able to begin to celebrate the ways in which they are different.

My own experience of growing up in Belfast taught me from an early age that society's reaction to difference is all too often devastating and destructive. It is my hope and belief that the brave and tireless efforts of the men and women working for peace – both now and in the past – will mean that celebrating diversity one day becomes possible for those currently divided by their ethnic and cultural differences.

Nowhere is the new sense of cordiality and trust between Britain and Ireland more important than in the constructive way in which our governments are working together towards achieving sustainable peace in Northern Ireland. It is also important to recognise here the considerable contribution that the United States of America has made to the success of the Peace Process to date. If Ireland and the UK are inextricably linked, the USA is surely the third point in a triangle of states bound by shared history and culture.

This is one reason why I am delighted that the British Council has decided to commission a second volume of essays on the topic of *Lives Entwined*, this time extending their invitation to some richly engaged Irish American contributors. In this volume, fresh explorations of this complex relationship also come from three professions which are close to my heart - the law, journalism and academe.

I hope these essays will have much to contribute towards an enriched understanding of all our similarities and differences – in Britain, in the USA, and here in Ireland.

Mary McAleese
PRESIDENT OF IRELAND

Tony Reilly
Director, British Council Ireland

Tony Reilly is currently Director of the British Council Ireland. He took up this post in July 2002 after previous postings with the British Council in South Africa, Turkey, Kuwait and Oman. He commissioned Through Irish Eyes *in 2003–a piece of extensive quantitative and qualitative research carried out by Behaviour & Attitudes to investigate changing Irish attitudes towards the UK among the Irish successor generation. He also commissioned the first volume of* Britain & Ireland: Lives Entwined *in 2005, a series of essays reflecting on the relationships between the two countries. With an Irish father, English mother, Irish wife and three children born respectively in Greece, Oman and Turkey, the issues of hybridity and national identity are never far from home. He has a first degree in Sociology and English, a Postgraduate Certificate in Education from Goldsmith's College London and an RSA Diploma in Teaching English as a Foreign Language.*

Introduction
Tony Reilly

Entwined or Entangled?

Three years ago, the British Council and the British Embassy jointly commissioned an extensive piece of attitudinal research (*Through Irish Eyes*). In the time-honoured tradition of discourse on Anglo–Irish relations, the results were presented, examined, picked over and hotly contested at the historic Mansion House in Dublin, in February 2004. The report argued that we were in the midst of some form of post-colonial recalibration in British–Irish relations. Proceeding with caution, it began to examine this largely benign and 'for-the-better' shift towards a more normal and equitable stage in what John Hume has called 'the totality of relationships between these islands'. In the process, we appear to have let a certain cat out of the bag – a hybrid and shadowy creature whose colours and nuances had not previously been identifiable. On first sighting, very different writers and thinkers were similarly entranced: willing to surface, to disentangle – and of course, contest – the uniquely complex, highly nuanced and often contradictory indicators that now began to reveal themselves under the headings of Anglo–Irish or British–Irish relations. Our first volume of *Britain & Ireland: Lives Entwined* essays, published in 2005, was the result.

With the slightest encouragement, a group of writers were eager to tap into the enormously rich and varied seam of their personal and professional insights to shed further light on this complex shift in relations. The first volume seemed to offer a space. Its title – *Britain & Ireland: Lives Entwined* – was taken from an essay by Cork-based academic and former Irish Foreign Service diplomat Piaras MacEinri. In his essay, Piaras, like many of his fellow contributors to the first (and this second) book, brought an impressive lucidity to his unravelling of the fluidity of notions of Britishness and Irishness. Content to leave questions unanswered and contradictions unresolved, his personal conclusion, however understated, was the opening of a new prospect. Perhaps at the end of the day, he muses, 'there is a bit of the British in the Irish and Irish in the British'. This possibility lies at the heart of both volumes.

Nevertheless the phrase 'lives entwined' has evoked some interesting responses across both volumes. Edna Longley was the first to point out, with a characteristically sharp eye for language, that entwine is a benign metaphor, with listed synonyms such as 'braid', 'interlace', 'embrace', 'plait' and 'weave'. She went on to suggest that such a phrase enshrined altogether too optimistic a view of the web of relations we had set out in these books to understand – a view that, in the new cosy romance between the old Lion and the young Tiger, factored out, or simply chose to ignore, the elephant in the room that is Northern Ireland. We were forced to ask ourselves if, swept away on the euphoric tide of improvements to British–Irish relations, we were indeed starting to believe our own propaganda and the rhetoric of greater trust, mutual understanding and relative psychological equivalence, which has become an article of hope and faith between our two countries. Is it a rose-tinted view that, even for a moment, sets aside the 'unfinished business' on this island, the legacy of a sordid armed conflict, the price of partition and the very real and evident challenges of reconciliation?

This second volume brings a new suggestion – that a more apt title for a book on Britain and Ireland might be 'Lives Entangled'. Imagine, instead of the linked arms of apple trees featured on the cover designed for the first volume by one of *The Guardian's* finest political cartoonists, Andrzej Krause, a much thornier and more barbed image, tightly enmeshed rather than gently interwoven, and impossibly knotted rather than comfortably braided. I hope the range and diversity of views across both volumes has not swept too much of history, or its legacies, under the carpet. It would be a mistake to reduce the drama of British–Irish history and identity into some overly simplistic portrait of blissful harmony and mutual understanding. The devil lies in the detail, in the challenge to express the inexpressibly complex, and contradictory, dynamics that have been deeply at play for so many centuries.

On, swiftly then, to this second volume of 10 essays – *Britain & Ireland: Lives Entwined II*. Why commission another book? What are our aspirations for this collection? Three broad aims prompted this follow-up collection.

First, we simply wanted more. We knew the seam remained tantalisingly untapped, and we have developed a taste for the rich mix of personal anecdote and reflective analysis contributors seem willing and eager to offer, whether they are journalists, politicians, civil servants, sportsmen, academics, lawyers or civil rights activists.

Second, this gave us more of a chance to widen the range of views and voices, to offer readers a plethora of perspectives, shaped and differentiated by gender, geography, generation, profession, family influence, worldview, personal philosophy and individual conditions of existence. The views and contributions contained in both volumes do not constitute a British Council view on any of the issues covered. But our role, as an independent broker of conversations about Britain and Ireland, must be to seek them out, not to limit or constrain particular viewpoints. It is not our intention, either implicitly or explicitly, to endorse or challenge any of the tones taken or arguments made in either book. It is our intention to convene and create a safe space for these discussions to be aired.

And third, in this second volume we have introduced to the mix a transatlantic perspective on Anglo–Irish relations. At the end of the introduction to the first *Lives Entwined*, I alluded to the 'special relationships' with the USA that both the UK and Ireland are said to enjoy, hinting that this triangular set of relationships might warrant further investigation. Are there features in common in these special relationships, or are their origins quite different? More crucially, the history and culture overlapping between these three predominantly English-speaking nations has exerted a profound and enduring influence on British–Irish relations. How did this come about? What is the nature of Irish America today? What is 'the American connection', as one of our contributors puts it, and how precisely does it work? How true are the myths that persist around the 44 million Americans who claim Irish ethnic ancestry? And what about the 33 million US citizens who claim English ancestry? What is America's take on, and stake in, the recent shifts in the tectonic plates that make up the archipelago of Britain and Ireland?

Ronald Reagan, the Kennedys, Bill Clinton, George Mitchell and George Bush have consistently invested considerable resources, time and political energy in Ireland – why is this? The USA provided vital inspiration and support in the 1960s and 1970s for the civil rights movement in Northern Ireland. US engagement with, and commitment to, the peace process over the years has stayed strong and resolute despite Ireland's neutrality during the First and Second World Wars, largely undeterred by the war against terror, and unaffected by the tacit acceptance of an increasingly close and special relationship between London and Washington. Another of our US-based contributors suggests a possible answer: 'Britain and Ireland together gave birth to Irish America – in all its hues.' Tracking the historical and diasporic links across the Atlantic adds a fresh, intriguing dimension to this second volume.

These 18 essays – 10 in the second volume plus the eight contributions in the first – together open up an intricate web of relations between two sets of people that pushes the adjective 'entwined' to its limits: knotted, entangled and inextricably interwoven, this already extremely rich cultural tapestry is further illuminated by the American connection. It should come as no surprise, therefore, that across both books a multiplicity of often diametrically opposed views and analyses of British–Irish relations emerge.

Tying up the loose ends is not on our agenda. As Piaras MacEinri wisely reminded us – there's nothing neat and tidy about history. So we are left with more questions posed than answered, more dilemmas presented than resolved, more contradictions exposed than arguments won, more ambiguity and less clarity. Some of the key questions opened up by these essays concern what lies ahead. Is the future bright and hopeful, or dim and gloomy? Has the grace and spirit of the Belfast/Good Friday Agreement opened up new possibilities to unite hearts and minds – putting territorial claims on the back-burner for now? Or do sectarianism and political polarisation make the prospects for Northern Ireland pretty bleak, notwithstanding a halt to the worst of the violence? Has membership of Europe and Ireland's renewed self-confidence on the back of the Celtic Tiger given rise to a genuine sense of parity and psychological equivalence between Britain and Ireland? Or are we guilty, in this new era of cordiality, of sweeping too many issues under the carpet – including an abiding asymmetry in relations between big Britain and its much smaller neighbour on the western fringes of Europe?

The tapestry that is British–Irish cultural relations is uniquely complex. Whether the historical intermingling of people and the passage of time has enabled us to reach a softer phase, where differences are more comfortably accommodated, shared agendas and cultural reference points more openly acknowledged, and entrenched animosities and historical baggage more readily parked, appears to depend on the lens through which one looks. Some of our contributors are comfortable with a more benign treatment or interpretation of our interwoven past and present. For others, the glass remains half empty. Their informed experience of our intermingled history and identity is much thornier, more entangled and intractable. One of our writers draws on the wisdom of an old woman in her assessment that it may take three generations for the scars of conflict and division to heal, and for trust and empathy to take root. For another writer, the process of rapprochement is well under way, with two key upcoming events symbolic of this – the visit in February 2007 by the English Rugby team to one of the spiritual homes of Irish nationalism, the Gaelic Athletic Association's Croke Park; and the much anticipated and, according to many commentators, now eagerly awaited first state visit of a British monarch to the sovereign Republic of Ireland.

For the younger Irish generation – *The Pope's Children* (David McWilliams, 2005, Gill & Macmillan), the successor or successful generation or, as one of our contributors refers to them, the 'hybrid generation' – narrow forms of nationalism have less and less relevance these days. The hybrid generation are more at ease with multiple or compound identities: they can live with being British and Irish, European and Irish, British and Asian, American and Irish, Polish and Irish, and so on. It needn't be either/or.

In closing, I hope readers of this and the previous volume of essays finish up both as confused and as clear as I am about the knotty complexity of cultural relations within and between Britain and Ireland. I also hope that these essays make a small contribution towards a deeper appreciation and understanding, on all sides, of this complexity. Nothing is straightforward about *Lives Entwined* – or should it be *Entangled*?

John Bruton

John Bruton is the EU Commission's Ambassador to the United States. A former Taoiseach, his government (1994–97) provided strong economic growth, advanced the Northern Irish Peace Process, and chaired a much admired EU Presidency (1996). His European credentials also include helping to draft the first European Constitution. Bruton got an early start in national politics when he was elected to the Irish Parliament in 1969 for the Fine Gael Party at the age of 22. He became Party Leader in 1990 and took Fine Gael into government in 1994. He has held several ministerial positions including Finance (1981–82 and 1986–87); Industry and Energy (1982–83); and Trade, Commerce and Tourism (1983–86). He successfully contested every election since 1969, resigning his seat only to assume his diplomatic post in Washington. Born into a farming family, Bruton is a Bachelor of Arts graduate of University College Dublin, and a barrister. He is married to Finola Bruton and has four children.

A personal perspective on Ireland's relationship with Britain

John Bruton

My own life has been shaped by Anglo–Irish relations, directly and through my family, but also through my study of history. Pondering such historic events as the first important landmark in Ireland's progression towards independence, the Home Rule Act enacted into law on 18 September 1914; or the war for Irish independence launched by the IRA and the Treaty of 1921 which was its aftermath, I must question the usefulness of the contribution made by armed action to the cause of Ireland. Although the 26 counties gained a greater degree of independence in 1922 than was granted in 1914, they had to endure a guerilla war, reprisals, atrocities and a civil war. I believe that without any violence, Home Rule would have evolved towards Dominion status and that this, in turn, probably would have led peacefully towards full independence and towards separate Irish EU membership. Furthermore, Home Rule would have given better protection to the Nationalist minority in Northern Ireland because it involved a continued presence of Southern Nationalist MPs at Westminster.

I would also question the pursuit by Irish separatists of the holy grail of absolute sovereignty. Sharing of power is part of the human condition. It was ever a myth to say that any nation was fully sovereign. It was always limited by local and universal rules and customs, by supranational institutions such as the Church, and by the rights of others. The will o' the wisp of absolute sovereignty, pursued with such dedication by Irish republicans, was actually a notion promulgated by British imperialism in the nineteenth century, in its insistence on the absolute sovereignty of the Westminster Parliament. Its adoption as the ideal of Irish nationalism made a solution to the Northern Ireland problem more difficult.

I have come to the conclusion that violence, and the political cosseting of those who would use it, has always been destructive of the cause of true Irish freedom and unity. Violence requires no patience and no empathy with antagonists. I hope that some scenes from my life and times will show that now, as then, the achievement of Irish freedom and unity requires immense patience and a huge, empathetic effort to understand Unionism. It requires the overcoming of our own fears.

My first visit to Britain was as a very small child. I went over on the mail boat from Dun Laoghaire to Holyhead with my mother. We were visiting my aunt, who was a nun in the Bon Sauveur Convent there. My most vivid memory of the place itself is of being separated from my mother for a few short seconds in a shop. The experience of travelling over on the mail boat, the 'Queen Maud', was thrilling. At that time thousands of Irish people were taking the mail boat to Holyhead, never to return, seeking work in England because there was none at home. As a small child I was not aware of the deep sadness that so many of my fellow passengers must have felt as the coast of Ireland disappeared over the horizon.

I was born in 1947 to a farming family in County Meath. My family were (and still are) involved in the cattle business. They bought store cattle in the West of Ireland, brought them to maturity and sold them to the British market. My father was one of four brothers working as business partners in the Maynooth/Dunboyne area. More than any other class of people, the cattle producers were directly and immediately affected by the ups and downs of Ireland's relationship with Britain.

During the First World War cattle prices were high because Britain was at war, its soldiers were at the front, and they needed Irish beef for nourishment. When the war ended, cattle prices inevitably fell. Farm workers' wages, which had risen during the wartime labour shortage, suddenly looked unaffordable. There followed a farm workers' strike, or more accurately a lock-out, which left a residue of bitterness in the cultural life of Meath and other eastern counties that took generations to erase. Such were the effects of fluctuations of Ireland's trading relationship with Britain.

Indeed, the economic 'war' of the 1930s between Britain and Ireland had already affected the way our family looked at the world. This 'war' was a direct result of Éamon de Valera's policy decision to cease paying land annuities to Britain that were owing to the British tax payer. The then joint British–Irish Treasury had put up the money to buy out the Irish landlords in the period 1880–1903, and annuities were payable to Britain under the terms of the 1921 Treaty. But de Valera had not accepted that Treaty.

When he started to withhold the land annuities in 1933, the British Government decided to close the British market to Irish exports. At that time, the overwhelming bulk of Irish exports to Britain were agricultural, and mainly in the form of cattle. Of the 4 million cattle produced in Ireland in 1930, a large proportion went to Britain. So when the British market closed there was a disastrous fall in the price of cattle in Ireland, and cattle were Ireland's biggest export. This hit farming families like my own exceptionally hard. As I was growing up, the memory of calves having to be destroyed because there was no market for them was something that was both fresh and bitter among my relatives. It coloured attitudes to de Valera, and blinded many people to such virtues as he had.

Later many Irish people, including my own family, might have admired Éamon de Valera's ability to keep Ireland out of the Second World War. They were not particularly happy with his introduction of compulsory tillage on land that had not been ploughed since the 1840s, as part of the war effort. But as sea traffic was being torpedoed, Ireland could no longer feed itself with imported grain.

My father was the brother put in charge of tilling the pasture to comply with the law: not exactly a place of family honour, given the visceral detestation that many grass farmers felt towards ploughing up land at all. But it was a blessing in disguise, because it enabled him to develop his distinctive skills and to put his mechanical talents to use in a way that would never have been possible had he confined his experience to buying, feeding, judging and selling cattle.

In the 1950s and early 1960s, my father became very actively involved in the National Farmers' Association (NFA), campaigning for Irish entry to the European Common Market. Agricultural prices were much better on the continent than in Britain, the only market then open to Irish cattle exporters. So that they could sell their cattle more cheaply into their own market, the British operated a deficiency payments system whereby British farmers were paid money directly. Irish cattle exporters, and the Irish farmers who depended on them to buy their cattle, did not qualify. The market was thus artificially skewed to disadvantage the Irish farmer for the benefit of British consumers and farmers. One of my father's campaigns in the NFA was to try to have this policy changed. This involved visits to Britain and talks with the British Farmers' Union and with British officials. These efforts were largely futile: Britain continued to pursue what would now be seen as a trade-distorting policy.

Hence the strong support among the farming community for efforts by such politicians as Sean Lemass and James Dillon to reduce dependency on Britain by achieving Irish membership of the European Common Market. To that end, my father went on an NFA study tour of the European continent. My first introduction to 'Europe' was through the colour slide pictures he brought home and showed to everyone willing to sit down and look at them. I could trace my later fascination with the European continent to viewing those slides over and over again. Around this time, I was beginning to develop an interest of my own in public life.

Public life

My first personal memory of politics is of hearing General Sean McEoin, 'The Blacksmith of Ballinalee', speak in the 1950s in Newbridge, Co. Kildare, as part of his unsuccessful campaign for the Presidency of Ireland. While our family had no overt political associations, they were in the constitutional nationalist tradition rather than in the republican tradition. My grand-uncle had been a staunch admirer of John Redmond and had filled the house in which I now live with memorabilia of that great Irish leader, including detailed contemporaneous newspaper accounts of his funeral in April 1918.

At school in Clongowes, I joined the An Fórsa Cosanta Áitiúil (FCÁ, the local defence force), and was a member of D company of the 20th battalion operating out of Griffith Barracks. This consisted of secondary school students from schools in and around Dublin. Most of the drilling happened locally at the weekends. But in the summer we went on camp for 2 weeks' training to the barracks in Kilkenny. This, in some senses, was a free holiday. We got lots of fresh air, an opportunity to use weapons, and occasional bouts of wild socialising in the city of Kilkenny. Overall, very pleasant. But I did notice, as a participant in the FCA guard of honour outside the post office on the 50th Anniversary of the 1916 Rising, that many young men from other schools had far more nationalistic viewpoints than I would have been used to hearing. Among some of my FCA companions there was a strong sense of Britain as the enemy. I was more than conscious of the defects of Britain's relationship with Ireland, but never in my life had I felt any general feeling of anti-Britishness.

As a schoolboy growing up in the 1950s, I was influenced by two big forces present in the cultural life of the Republic of Ireland: the Catholic faith and Irish nationalism. In retrospect it is hard to see how these two influences coexisted so easily in Ireland at that time. Catholicism is and was, both by its name and its nature, universalist. If Catholics adhered to the faith, they should regard all people no matter what their nationality or race as of equal value. Irish nationalism, on the other hand, was particularist. Only people who had the right background qualified as being true Gaels. There had indeed been a lot of talk in Irish nationalist circles about the 'Irish race' until that sort of phraseology had been made unfashionable by events on the continent of Europe. I remember asking myself what choice I would make if I were forced to choose between my religious and my national beliefs. For much of my youth I felt that national loyalty would have the stronger pull. But, as life wore on, I came to change that view.

I became National Secretary of the Fine Gael Youth Group in 1966, just as the troubles in Northern Ireland were beginning. Inspired by the non-violent civil rights movement of Martin Luther King in the USA, Nationalists in Northern Ireland started to agitate peacefully for an end to gerrymandering of constituencies and to discrimination in housing and employment. Unfortunately, the response to the civil rights movement from hard-line Unionists was far from non-violent.

That was all something of a shock for me. My childhood image of Northern Ireland had been of a place that was distinctly better off than the Republic. You could get Mars bars in Northern Ireland, after all. Many of my mother's contemporaries took the train to Belfast because the range and quality of goods in the shops improved on what was available in Dublin. We people born after independence were so concerned with getting on with our own lives, and with getting our own State established on a decent footing, that we did not have much time to think about the divided loyalties in Northern Ireland. One of my school friends was from Warrenpoint, Co. Down, and one day when we were visiting Newry, we saw an Orange Parade. It all looked so quaint, unthreatening and almost funny to see men with colourful sashes and bowler hats walking down the street. I thought to make a joke about this, but my friend suggested that I might be better advised to keep quiet. This was my first exposure to the realities of Northern Irish politics.

Some Southern politicians had, of course, trumpeted 'United Ireland' as a particularly useful rallying cry, because it had the special merit of having both a strong emotional charge and little prospect of being achieved. It was therefore constantly recyclable

The goal of restoration of the Irish language as the principal spoken language of the country was also in that category. It was never going to be achieved, but few would have the courage to say so: to be against promoting the Irish language by compulsion was to be 'pro-British', and in those times few wanted to be seen to be that. The Language Freedom Movement (LFM) of the 1960s challenged this dogma, seeking to remove the artificial preference given to those who did their exams using Irish, and to allow students a choice, after their Intermediate Certificate, to give up Irish in favour of other subjects. The LFM was subject to virulent criticism, exposing a deeply unattractive level of intolerance in conventional thinking in Ireland at that time. A number of Fine Gael politicians such as James Dillon and Paddy Belton gave them courageous support, and that would have increased my affinity with that party.

When Irish nationalism developed in the nineteenth century, it faced a major ideological difficulty in accommodating itself to the existence of a large, concentrated minority of people in north-east Ulster who did not share its aspirations of separation from Britain. With an innocence that prevailed in some quarters until very recent times, Irish nationalists reassured themselves that, once Britain was out of the way, all that was necessary was for Nationalists and Unionists to sit down together for a few days and all these differences could easily be sorted out.

None of the great Irish Nationalist leaders, from O'Connell, through Parnell, to Griffith and de Valera, formulated a policy that would win Unionists over to support the nationalist cause. They did not even try. Nationalists focused their attention instead on the British, and on forcing Britain to concede Home Rule or independence to Ireland. Rather than winning Unionists over to support an agreed project for a more independent Ireland, as de Valera put it, Unionists must either accept that they were part of the Irish nation or else proclaim themselves an English garrison. That was as constructive as it got!

I was elected to Dáil Éireann (the Parliament of the Irish Republic) in June 1969. My parliamentary career has coincided with what has loosely been described as the 'Troubles' in Northern Ireland. The years since 1969 have seen successive efforts to 'solve' the problem, and also major shifts in attitudes towards what the problem actually is.

Dormant passions

Apart from sporadic campaigns against partition, public opinion in the Republic between 1922 and 1967 largely ignored events in Northern Ireland until the people there began to take things into their own hands.

The first civil rights march was organised in August 1968 by Austin Currie, later a colleague of mine in Dail Éireann. In particular, he was protesting against discrimination against Catholics in housing. Subsequent civil rights marches led to Unionist counter-demonstrations and confrontations with police. Television images of police, showing the batoning of civil rights demonstrators in Derry, radicalised nationalist opinion throughout Ireland. In 1969 an organisation called People's Democracy, claiming it was modelled on the 1965 American civil rights march from Selma to Montgomery, organised a march from Belfast to Derry without the backing or approval of the Northern Ireland Civil Rights Association. The way the marchers were attacked by Loyalists and undefended by the police unearthed layers of animosity on both sides of the divide that had lain partly buried for decades. As a result, although almost all the internal reforms sought by civil rights campaigners were eventually granted, these came at the cost of further polarising relations between Catholics and Protestants in Northern Ireland. These attacks on Catholics led to the formation of the Provisional IRA, initially as a defensive organisation.

There is still controversy about the extent to which members of the then Fianna Fáil Government in Dublin in 1969–70 were involved in using public money to give initial finance and arms to the Provisional IRA. As far as Northern Ireland was concerned, there was very little coherence or internal control within that Government. I recall the fierce controversy that these allegations engendered. I was a young Member of the Dáil at the time, and we sat continuously day and night for almost 40 hours, inconclusively debating what had happened. Passions dormant since the Civil War of the 1920s re-emerged.

Following that catharsis, the Irish Government came to take a much more considered and controlled approach to the Northern problem, recognising that there were two sides to it, and that a sovereign government could never allow itself to become allied to private or illegal armies, whatever it thought of their long-term goals. Ministers for Justice, such as Des O'Malley and Pat Cooney, showed notable courage in their opposition to the IRA.

Meanwhile the IRA moved onto the offensive, with the aim of bringing down the local Unionist administration. The following year, 1971, the IRA campaign reached such an intensity that the Unionist Prime Minister of Northern Ireland, with the reluctant assent of the British Government, introduced internment without trial of 452 'suspects'. Only 342 were actually apprehended, and many were quickly released because they were totally uninvolved with any illegality.

In the rioting that followed internment, thousands were left homeless. Catholics and Protestants in mixed areas left their homes, creating the segregation and misnamed 'peace lines' between neighbourhoods that continue to this day in much of Belfast. One such 'peace line' in the Ardoyne has recently been in the news because it passes through the grounds of a Catholic school.

But the most radicalising event of all for nationalists was the 'Bloody Sunday' shootings of January 1972, when 13 unarmed demonstrators were shot by the British Army.

The reaction of Nationalists to this bloody event was encapsulated by John Hume in the uncharacteristic words 'many people feel now that it is a United Ireland or nothing'. The hopeful dawn of the civil rights movement had been erased. The British Army, which had initially been welcomed by Catholics as a protection against Loyalists, had come to be seen as an enemy. I remember the black flags of mourning and anger displayed outside my own church in

Dunboyne after Bloody Sunday. Previously uninvolved people, who I knew well, were swept by these emotions into the Republican movement and into support for its violent campaign of revenge. Things had changed for the worse.

Every subsequent victim of violence is, or was, a parent, a child, a close relative or a work colleague of 30 or 40 other people. When someone close to you is a victim of political violence, it changes your perception of events. From the time I first became a member of the Dáil in 1969 up to 1973, I shared a small office with another young TD from my neighbouring county of Monaghan, Billy Fox. Billy Fox, one of the few Protestants in the Dáil, was murdered by the IRA on 11 March 1974. I have never forgotten the horror of that event, something that enables me to understand, in a small way, the feelings of the friends and family of all victims of political violence.

I also felt for the victims of Bloody Sunday: 24 years later, as Taoiseach, I initiated the official study of all the evidence by my officials, which led directly to the current Tribunal of Enquiry into that tragedy.

Steps on the road

Bloody Sunday led, pretty directly, to the ending by the British Government of the local Unionist administration of Northern Ireland. There followed the first major attempt to find a comprehensive solution to the problem – involving Nationalists in government as well as Unionists for the first time. The British Government published a white paper, in March 1973, which called for power-sharing and an 'Irish dimension'. This 'Irish dimension' was negotiated at Sunningdale.

Brian Faulkner, Leader of the Unionist Party, reluctantly accepted these proposals as a price for getting some kind of local administration re-established. He took the view, similar to that taken in more recent times by David Trimble, that sharing power with local Nationalists was better than having no local power at all. But, like David Trimble, he had a precarious hold on his Party. Two days before the power-sharing executive was set up in November 1973, Faulkner's own Ulster Unionist Council accepted power-sharing by the narrowest margin – 379 votes to 369. Faulkner, like Trimble, was a risk-taker.

At Sunningdale, Brian Faulkner and the Unionists were hoping that they would get the Irish Government to extradite the IRA suspects for trial in Northern Ireland, and to change the constitution of the Republic to amend Articles 2 and 3, which claimed Irish sovereignty over the territory of Northern Ireland. Northern Nationalists and the Irish Government, on the other hand, wanted a strong all-Ireland body – a Council of Ireland – that would develop dynamically in power and scope, and be capable of being presented as a substantial move in the direction of a United Ireland. They also wanted the reform of the Royal Ulster Constabulary (RUC) – the Northern Ireland Police, which had been accused of pro-Unionist bias in its security operations.

In my view, the Sunningdale negotiators did not take enough notice of the weakness of Brian Faulkner's political position. He got no amendment of the Irish Constitution – only a political declaration that there could be no change in the status of Northern Ireland without majority agreement there. This was heralded by some as a major advance, but was little more than a statement of pragmatic political and military reality. Faulkner got no move on extradition, beyond an inoperable arrangement to try would-be extraditees in the Republic. In return, he conceded a Council of Ireland which, because it would only operate by unanimity, would probably not have done very much at all, but which looked frightening to grassroots Unionists.

So when a British General Election was called just 3 months later, the result destroyed the political base of Brian Faulkner and the Unionists, who had supported power-sharing and the Sunningdale Agreement. Anti-Sunningdale Unionists got 51% of the total vote, while Pro-Sunningdale Unionists got only 13%. The democratic mandate for Sunningdale from the Unionist side was destroyed. Faulkner did not give up straight away. He persisted, initially even in the teeth of a paralysing strike organised by the Ulster Workers' Council. But the British Government was unwilling to put the military in on a sufficient scale to break the strike and run essential services. Without adequate British support, Faulkner resigned and the agreement collapsed.

As a Junior Minister in the Irish Government at that time, meeting my counterpart in the short-lived power-sharing executive, Ivan Cooper, to discuss how our respective sports policies could be coordinated, I remember the high hopes that a new era was about to dawn. The shock of the collapse in the face of the Ulster Workers' Council strike was accentuated by the naïve euphoria that had preceded it.

Why did it all go wrong? What lessons could the collapse of the Sunningdale Agreement have taught us in the negotiation and implementation of the Good Friday Agreement in 1998? First, as I said, Faulkner's Unionists were asked to carry too heavy a burden in light of their political position. Second, everything agreed at Sunningdale was provisional. Everyone could keep their 'aspirations' and continue to work for something better for themselves. In the zero-sum politics of Northern Ireland, that always meant something less for someone else. To employ Middle East parlance, there were no 'final-status negotiations' at Sunningdale. Some felt they were on a slippery slope, and nobody made their last possible concession, because the deal was so structured that they could always ask for more; or, in the Unionist case, be asked for more.

The lack of any 'final - status negotiation' is a problem with the Good Friday Agreement of 1998 as well. It is provisional rather than permanent, a step on a road rather than a destination. And that deprives it of the full commitment that some should give it.

This sense of sliding in one direction only is part of the continuing insecurity of Unionists to this day. It partly explains irrational, sometimes despicable, actions such as the intimidation of schoolchildren in the Ardoyne. It also explains the Unionist obsession with symbols, flags, emblems and parades. Irish nationalists have yet to come up with any comprehensive response to these deep Unionist feelings of insecurity. Nationalists have not tried to do so, because they want to hold onto their own aspirations for an unqualified sovereign United Ireland. The obsession on the part of both Nationalists and Unionists with territorial sovereignty, a nineteenth-century notion, continues to do its damage.

The disastrous collapse of Sunningdale and power-sharing meant that no serious attempt was made at a comprehensive settlement, involving local politicians, for a long time thereafter. Northern Ireland descended into a long valley of violence, confrontation, increasing sectarianism and hunger strikes. The British security forces and the IRA fought one another to a standstill and, in terms of creative thinking, local politics within Northern Ireland itself stood still too.

Agreements and declarations

When I became Leader of the main opposition Party, Fine Gael, in late 1990, I made the building of bridges to Unionism one of my priorities. I indicated a willingness on Fine Gael's part to change Articles 2 and 3 of the Irish Constitution. In early November 1993, just a month before the Downing Street Declaration, I was the first-ever leader of any party in the South, in over 70 years, to meet the Ulster Unionist Party in their Belfast headquarters in Glengall Street. Our delegation was shown around the building by David Trimble, who proudly showed us copies of the Ulster Covenant of 1912, and Unionist posters from elections long ago. I regard this visit as an important step in rebuilding a bridge between the Republic and the Unionists that had been broken by the way in which the Anglo–Irish Agreement had been negotiated.

I had been a member of the Irish Government at the time of the Anglo–Irish Agreement where, instead of directly involving the local politicians, the two governments, one led by Garret FitzGerald and the other by Margaret Thatcher, negotiated over their heads. I had expressed concern in Cabinet that there was a lack of symmetry between the levels of consultation of Nationalists and of Unionists in the working out of the Agreement, and that this could lead to problems afterwards. It did. But there may have been no alternative.

The immediate effect of the Agreement on Unionists, however, had been cataclysmic. There was a huge demonstration in Belfast. The Unionist Leader Jim Molyneaux described his community's reaction as one of 'universal cold fury'. But there was no repeat of the Ulster Workers' Strike of 1974. Why? Probably because, whereas in 1974 they were confronting a weak Labour Government and could hope to appeal to the Unionism of the then Conservative opposition, in 1985 Unionists were dealing directly with Margaret Thatcher, an avowed Unionist herself, whose Labour opposition replacement would have been even less palatable to Unionists. A repeat of the Ulster Workers' Strike would have been met with the same steely resolve on Mrs Thatcher's part as the British coal miners faced.

In my view, the primary benefit of the Anglo–Irish Agreement lay in the dramatic improvement it heralded in the relationship between the British and Irish governments. Whenever subsequent differences arose about particular events, a ready-made mechanism existed for discussing them. A safety valve was created, and megaphone diplomacy became unnecessary.

This visit to Glengall Street by a major Southern party may also have contributed a little to ensuring that the subsequent Unionist reaction to the Downing Street Declaration was as calm as it was. The Downing Street Declaration differed from the Anglo–Irish Agreement in that, this time, the Ulster Unionist leadership was properly consulted by the British Government. In contrast to his reaction to the Anglo–Irish Agreement, the Unionist Leader Jim Molyneaux said the Declaration was 'not a sell-out'. He thus severed a common front with Dr Paisley of the Democratic Unionist Party (DUP). Gerry Adams of Sinn Féin did not reject the Declaration either, but looked instead for 'clarification'.

What also differentiated the Downing Street Declaration of 1993 from previous efforts is that it explicitly set out with a goal of bringing into mainstream politics parties that had been, and are to this day, associated with illegal paramilitary or terrorist organisations. Previous efforts, both at Sunningdale and in the Anglo–Irish Agreement, were directed only at parties that had constitutionalist credentials, however radical their other disagreements. The paramilitaries had been ignored.

The British Government undertook, in the Downing Street Declaration, to introduce legislation to facilitate a United Ireland if that became the wish of both North and South. There was, however, no complementary provision for a possible reversal of that decision, once taken. This was an 'optional one-way street' on sovereignty over Northern Ireland. To have made the street a two-way one would have undermined the aim of getting the IRA to stop violence.

The strategy, originating with John Hume, was (a) to get the British to become neutral on the issue of whether Northern Ireland remained in the UK or joined a United Ireland; and (b) to satisfy Sinn Féin and the IRA that, if a new agreement was approved in simultaneous referenda in both North and South, this would meet their demand for Irish 'national self-determination'. It was far short of British withdrawal – the traditional Sinn Féin/IRA demand on self-determination.

In November 1990, Peter Brooke had stated that Britain had no 'selfish strategic or economic interest in Northern Ireland', thereby meeting Hume's first condition. In the Declaration, the British Government agreed that it was for the people of Ireland alone 'to exercise their right of self-determination on the basis of consent, freely and concurrently given, North and South, to bring about a United Ireland, if that is their wish'. The Downing Street Declaration aimed to create the conditions for such talks.

It is important to note that the Declaration referred to a 'permanent' end to the use of, and support for, violence. It did not refer to a mere ceasefire which, by its nature, is potentially temporary. The Declaration therefore reflected the view of the governments that good faith negotiations would be possible only if all parties were on a level playing field. A party that was associated with a private army, which might resume military operations, would not be on a level playing field with a party that had no such army. That was why the word 'permanent' in the Downing Street Declaration was important.

It took the IRA 8 months after the Downing Street Declaration to decide on what it called 'a complete cessation of military operations'. Despite the fact that the IRA had studied the Downing Street Declaration carefully, and would have seen that a permanent end to violence was what it required, there was no reference at all in the IRA statement to the cessation being 'permanent', 'irreversible', 'intended to be permanent', or any other synonym that would have met the requirements of the Declaration. The IRA said only that they would stop what they called 'military operations', as distinct from the more comprehensive term – 'violence' – used in the Downing Street Declaration.

Attempts were made afterwards to say that a 'complete' cessation meant the same thing as a 'permanent' cessation, but this was blatantly not so. The subsequent difficulties about the decommissioning of IRA weapons arose directly from this ambiguity in the original IRA statement. Sinn Féin and the IRA repeatedly refused to say that the IRA's cessation was permanent.

Although Sinn Féin pretended it was a new 'precondition' to talks, the notion of an initial gesture of decommissioning weapons was only put forward by the British as a weak alternative to an IRA statement that the ceasefire was permanent, so that Sinn Féin could come into round-table talks with the governments without having complied with the actual terms of the Downing Street Declaration.

It surprised me, when I became Taoiseach in December 1994, a year after the Downing Street Declaration and 3 months after the IRA's cessation statement, that the conditions on which Sinn Féin were to be allowed into talks while the IRA still retained the means to go back to violence had not been sorted out. Wasn't it a strange thing for Albert Reynolds and John Major to have left so vague in the contacts their intermediaries had with Sinn Féin, either around the time of the Downing Street Declaration in the previous year, or before the IRA's cessation announcement 3 months earlier? This omission by the principals and their intermediaries has never been explained.

The failure to clarify that issue left a structural flaw in the process that remains to this day. It would have been possible to defer the issue of actual decommissioning if the word 'permanent' had been used in the IRA cessation statement. But, in the absence of such a declaration of intent, the weapons themselves inevitably became politically central. Those who drafted the IRA cessation statement of 1994 must have known that.

My own feeling, and I expressed this concern at the time, is that the problem lay in the fact that the Republican leadership simply did not tell their own grassroots frankly about what they were doing between 1993 and 1995. They may even have told them the opposite. They may even have pretended to their grassroots that the ceasefire was intended to be temporary, while suggesting to everyone else that it was intended to be permanent. Constructive ambiguity has limits.

Patience is a virtue

Such obfuscations caused difficulties in the peace process after I took over from Albert Reynolds as Taoiseach in December 1994. Although the IRA was on ceasefire from August 1994 to February 1996, violence by them, as defined in the Downing Street Declaration, did not in fact stop. Notwithstanding this, my object as Taoiseach was to get Sinn Féin into talks with the other parties. I believed, wrongly as it transpired, that once the talks were moving forward productively, Sinn Féin and the IRA would avail themselves of one of several options they had to take the heat out of the decommissioning issue. The IRA did not take any of them.

In view of John Major's increasingly precarious majority in Westminster, and his need for the votes of Ulster Unionist MPs, the strategy we evolved was to deal with the decommissioning issue in parallel with the entry of Sinn Féin to the talks, rather than as a precondition to it. Eventually, at a Summit on 28 November 1995, on the eve of President Clinton's first visit to Ireland, John Major and I announced this twin-track approach. This was achieved in a succession of phone calls between John Major and myself in the hours before the Summit. I believe it was a huge breakthrough. We agreed that: (a) all-party talks, hopefully involving Sinn Féin, would start the following February; and (b) an independent international body to assess the decommissioning issue, headed by Senator George Mitchell, would be set up straight away.

Senator Mitchell's group reported quickly, on 24 January 1996. They proposed six principles of non-violence to be met by parties taking part in the talks. These principles included the acceptance by parties of disarmament of paramilitary organisations, and of an end to punishment beatings. The Mitchell Group also said that they had received a clear commitment from all to work constructively to achieve full decommissioning 'from the paramilitaries' as part of the process of all-party negotiations.

Thirteen days after Senator Mitchell presented the report containing these words, the IRA ended its ceasefire altogether. Without advance security warning, it targeted the financial district of London in the Canary Wharf bomb on 5 February 1996 that murdered Inan Bashir and John Jeffries.

Why did they do it? Was Senator Mitchell told lies by the IRA? Was the commitment to 'work constructively' to achieve full decommissioning during the talks just a meaningless genuflection and, if that was all it was, why was it put in the Mitchell report at all? I believe that plain speaking would have been better.

Senator Mitchell does not address this in his book on the subject, *Making Peace* (Knopf, New York, 1999).

One account that does not convince me is that it was the suggestion of an election by John Major that prompted the IRA's decision to go back to war, barely a week after the presentation of the Mitchell report.

There is another possible explanation. Just a week before the IRA ended its ceasefire, all other parties in the Forum for Peace and Reconciliation in Dublin, including the Social Democratic and Labour Party (SDLP) and Fianna Fáil, adopted a report over Sinn Féin objections, which said that the consent of a majority in Northern Ireland was needed for any settlement to be viable. There was nothing new in this, but its formal enunciation in the Forum, and the consequent isolation of Sinn Féin, may have led the IRA to feel that they needed to detonate a bomb to get the 'pan-Nationalist front' back into line.

Notwithstanding the IRA's resumption of violence, John Major and I proceeded with our work to set in place a structure for all-party talks based on an electoral process. We set 10 June 1996 as the date for their commencement. We made the six Mitchell principles a requirement of participation. We initiated discussions on the format for elections. These discussions reached agreement on 21 March 1996. On 17 April, John Major and I agreed the ground rules on which this negotiating or talks body would operate.

In the days before polling day in the elections to the negotiating or talks body – 20 May 1996 – Sinn Féin said it would accept the Mitchell principles of non-violence. But the IRA campaign continued unabated, so obviously the IRA did not accept the Mitchell principles. Talks opened on 10 June 1996. Sinn Féin was not present because the IRA was still at war. The talks were prolonged and difficult in the period 1996–97. There was gamesmanship on the Unionist side, with Bob McCartney of the United Kingdom Unionist Party trying to upstage David Trimble. David Trimble could not be flexible on the ordering of the agenda until he had the British General Election of May 1997 behind him. Unionists wanted to deal with decommissioning first; Nationalists wanted it further down the agenda. But this did not take away from the fact that Unionists and Nationalists were, at least, sitting down with Irish and British

Ministers, for the first time since 1974, to negotiate the future together. The British General Election took place on 1 May 1997. David Trimble's position was strengthened, as his party's share of the vote held up well in comparison with that of Ian Paisley's DUP. A new government under Tony Blair won a clear majority, enabling it to act with a decisiveness that had been impossible for John Major.

I met Tony Blair in a summit meeting on 8 May. I put a number of proposals to him for intensified social and economic cooperation between Britain and Ireland, based on Labour's election programme. We also authorised continuing work on devising a joint formula to overcome the decommissioning hurdle. At a subsequent summit in New York, Tony Blair and I finalised proposals to provide for the establishment of: (a) an independent commission on weapons; and (b) a committee within the talks to deal with weapons in parallel with the political negotiations.

These proposals were put to the parties at the talks on 24 June 1997, and were the basis on which the talks subsequently moved forward to the Good Friday Agreement of 1998. With new governments in office in Dublin and London, the IRA declared a second ceasefire on 19 July 1997.

Two days after these proposals were put to the talks, I ceased to be Taoiseach and was replaced by the present incumbent, Bertie Ahern. Following the Irish General Election earlier that month, he had received the support of four independent deputies of the Dáil for a coalition government of his party, Fianna Fáil, and the Progressive Democrats, to replace the Fine Gael/Labour/Democratic Left Coalition that I had led from December 1994.

An unfinished story

An agreement was eventually reached – the Good Friday Agreement of 1998 – the terms of which are so well known that I do not need to describe them in full here. It was a significant achievement for George Mitchell and for all participants. The Good Friday Agreement was similar to the Sunningdale Agreement in many respects. For Nationalists, it was a mixed bag. It was less visibly ambitious on North/South issues and required a definitive amendment of Articles 2 and 3 of the Irish Constitution. But it was to prove to be more effective on police reforms. In any event, the differences between it and Sunningdale were so slight as to call into question once again the utility of the violence of the period 1974–97 from an Irish nationalist point of view. Just as in the case of 1916–21, there was not enough to show for all the suffering.

I remember visiting Stormont once the power-sharing executive had been re-established in May 2000, and being told by ministers of all parties how well they got on with ministers of other parties in doing business. I discovered, however, to my surprise, that the discussions between them were largely confined to official business or social chit-chat. The fundamental political problems, such as the unresolved questions of decommissioning and policing, were not being discussed at all between members of the Executive. They all seemed to have had the ability to compartmentalise things so that they could get on with some issues effectively, while ignoring others.

No progress, beyond further inspections of the arms dumps of the IRA, was made on the actual decommissioning of the weapons. In late October 2000, David Trimble was put in a difficult position at his Ulster Unionist Council by a motion from one of his colleagues to the effect that Sinn Féin should be expelled from the Executive unless the IRA decommissioned its weapons.

To prevent this motion being passed, David Trimble put forward an alternative proposal whereby Sinn Féin Ministers would be suspended from activity in the North/South bodies until decommissioning started. Sinn Féin deeply resented this move, which they regarded as a breach of the Good Friday Agreement. On the other hand, if Trimble had not made this proposal, the other motion would have been passed at the Ulster Unionist Council, and the consequences of that would have been more severe.

The fact that the Ulster Unionist Party, the SDLP and the DUP have now accepted the new police structures is a big step forward. But Gerry Adams has said that Catholics who join the new police service 'will be accorded the same treatment the Republican movement accorded the RUC. No more. No less'.

As I write, the story is not over. Although the challenges are formidable, there is a great emotional resilience in the peace process. There is also great tactical ingenuity among the participants. But other things are lacking across the island of Ireland.

One of these is a leap of imagination on the part of the Northern nationalists to think their way into the Unionist mind and find ways to assuage Unionist uncertainties. What is lacking on the Unionist side is a similar leap of imagination to see that they live in Ireland, and may make more reliable friends among their Nationalist neighbours and in Dublin than they will ever have in London.

What is lacking in Dublin is a willingness to step out of the sectarian grip of history and see that, as Britain's concerns move elsewhere, Dublin must act as a guarantor of Unionist rights just as much as it already does for Nationalists. The Irish Government must act in the interests of all the Irish people who live on the island, whether they describe themselves as 'Irish', 'British', 'Northern Irish', 'Ulster Scots' or anything else. That approach will wear down suspicion and slowly shake off the heavy burden of history.

Kevin Cullen

Kevin Cullen, a reporter for The Boston Globe, is a native of Boston, the grandson of Irish immigrants. He studied politics and history at Trinity College, Dublin, and began covering Northern Ireland after he joined the Globe in 1985. Over the next two decades he spent more time in Ireland than any reporter for an American newspaper; and had the unique perspective of covering the Anglo–Irish conflict while based in Dublin, London and Boston – the capital of Irish America. In 1997 he opened the Globe's Dublin bureau; and spent much of his time in Belfast covering the negotiations leading to the Good Friday Agreement. In 1998 he became the Globe's London bureau chief and European correspondent, spending as much time in the Balkans as in Belfast. He won a citation of excellence from the Overseas Press Club of America for interpretive reporting on Northern Ireland, and was a member of the Globe's investigative team that won the Pulitzer Prize for Public Service in 2003 for exposing the sexual abuse of children by Roman Catholic priests.

The American Connection
Kevin Cullen

When it comes to the Anglo–Irish peace process, the word 'historic' is thrown around a lot. The IRA ceasefire in 1994 was historic. Gerry Adams and Paddy Mayhew shaking hands was historic. Bill Clinton's visits to Belfast and Dublin were historic. The Good Friday Agreement was historic. The closure of the Maze Prison was historic. The IRA formally ending its armed campaign in July 2005 was historic.

These were all high-profile events, and history has duly recorded them. But there have been things that have taken place with little or no attention that suggest, as much as widely known milestones, that Anglo–Irish relations have really entered a new era.

i

In the summer of 2004, I was sitting at a dinner in the stately Beacon Hill home of John Rankin, Britain's Consul General in Boston. A delegation from the Democratic Unionist Party was in town, led by the party's deputy leader, Peter Robinson. I got talking with some of the younger DUP policy wonks at my table, and soon we were debating Greece's improbable run in the ongoing European football championship. 'You know,' I said, leaning forward, whispering conspiratorially, 'I know this pub...'

Twenty minutes later, me and the DUP fellows were standing in an Irish pub, watching the Euros on a widescreen TV. That DUP minions would be standing in an Irish pub in Boston, a city that their party leader, Dr Paisley, had repeatedly derided as an outpost of 'the Kennedy stable' of Irish America, showed just how much had changed, changed utterly. It seemed ... historic.

Dr Paisley, and not a few other Unionists, have long dismissed the USA as being hopelessly biased toward Nationalists. Stereotypes about Irish-Americans passing the hat around pubs to raise money for the IRA persisted throughout the Troubles, even though, like many stereotypes, that depiction was grossly exaggerated and not very representative of a huge bloc of people whose most defining characteristic is that they have no defining characteristic.

American attitudes about Ireland, especially Northern Ireland, are far more complex, complicated and nuanced than has generally been recognised. However dramatic it sounds to say that there are more than 40 million Americans of Irish descent, the reality is that many of them do not hail from Nationalist backgrounds, and the vast majority of them think that IRA stands for Individual Retirement Account.

It is true that Irish-Americans who are sympathetic to the Nationalist side have dominated the US debate about Ireland for more than a century. As the British and the Irish tussled over Ireland, the Irish diaspora in America always played a role, but its influence for both good and bad has tended to be exaggerated. And as the peace process unfolded, American attempts to be constructive and even-handed often were not recognised or appreciated.

Irish America was never as monolithic as its champions and critics portrayed it. For sure, there were some people who supported the IRA from the outset. But there was always something of a political disconnect between the IRA's supporters in Ireland and its stalwarts in places such as south Boston or Woodside in Queens. IRA supporters in Boston were scandalised in the 1970s when Bernadette Devlin visited and said she felt more comfortable with blacks in Roxbury than with conservative Irish-Americans in Southie. The domination of IRA support groups by older, conservative Irish-Americans prevented them from forming partnerships with younger, more radical activists in groups supporting revolution in Central America and South Africa, who would have been more natural IRA allies. Sympathy, and money, for the IRA spiked in the USA when the British were seen to have acted outrageously, such as when British troops shot 14 nationalists dead on Bloody Sunday in 1972; or when Margaret Thatcher allowed 10 Republican prisoners to die on hunger strike in 1981.

The money collected by IRA sympathisers attracted attention and admonishment from the American, British and Irish governments. But it was a pittance compared with the millions raised by American-based charities such as the American Ireland Fund, which was disbursed to those from both main traditions in Ireland. Contrary to popular opinion, the IRA didn't rely on American money or weapons. Republicans always coveted American political support far more than money or gear. And as the IRA campaign dragged on, the most influential Irish-Americans, especially politicians, distanced themselves from the IRA, even as many of those politicians continued to criticise British policy that they saw as perpetuating the conflict.

As the Troubles wore on, influential Irish Americans became more interested in effecting real change rather than professing allegiances. When he was speaker of the US House of Representatives, Tip O'Neill, the Massachusetts congressman who was the quintessential Irish-American pol, urged Ronald Reagan to encourage Thatcher to try something bold. In 1985 the Anglo–Irish Agreement, which gave Dublin a say in the affairs of Northern Ireland, became one of those vaunted 'historic' milestones. When Bill Clinton became the first non-veteran to be elected President since the end of the Second World War, he brought to the White House a post-Cold War paradigm in which the USA would not defer to its staunchest military ally on the issue of Northern Ireland. Clinton became involved in Northern Ireland not because he was a closet Nationalist, as some Unionists suspected at the time, but because he believed his administration could help resolve one of the world's conflicts that had been deemed intractable. Clearly, he wanted to reap the political benefits, if possible, but not from the supposed Irish-American voting bloc, because there is no evidence that Irish-Americans vote as a bloc. Clinton and his aides saw intervention in Northern Ireland in the same terms as they regarded intervention in Haiti and the Middle East. They wanted to make a difference, and be rewarded at the polls and recognised by posterity for doing so.

Still, old stereotypes fade slowly. In October 1994, when Loyalist leaders visited Boston shortly after calling their own ceasefire, they were stunned by the warm welcome they received in the most Irish of American cities. After speaking at Boston College, a Jesuit university founded by Irish immigrants in the 1860s, Joe English, a former loyalist paramilitary leader, sheepishly admitted his view of Irish America had been uninformed. 'I thought they were all Provos,' he said.

A year later, during the 'historic' conference on Northern Ireland at the Sheraton Hotel in Washington, DC, I introduced English to an old friend who had grown up in Belfast. When I asked my friend if he knew English, he replied, as he shook English's hand, 'Yeah, Joe's boys killed some of my friends.'

At the bar at the Sheraton, I introduced some loyalists to Courtney Kennedy, Bobby's daughter, who had married Paul Hill, one of the Guildford Four. They all exchanged handshakes, kisses, cigarettes and bottles of Heineken. In a hotel bar, 3000 miles away from where it all unfolded, the bitterness of conflict and the promise of a more peaceful era coexisted.

Watching supposed sworn enemies share the same space demonstrated the neutral ground that America constituted. Mainstream Unionists remained sceptical of American involvement long after Loyalists concluded that most Americans had neither an interest in, nor a preference as to whether Nationalists or Unionists would prevail in the power struggle in a post-conflict Northern Ireland.

American interest in Northern Ireland could be reduced to something as sweetly earnest as what I overheard a woman with an unmistakably southern drawl ask someone at the bar of the Sheraton Washington back in 1995: 'Would y'all just stop killing each other, please?'

George Mitchell's statesmanlike stewardship of the negotiations that concluded in the Good Friday Agreement did much to assuage suspicions that most Americans were closet Nationalists. But as a new millennium dawned, and Mitchell kept being dragged back to Belfast to help sort out one stalemate or another, there was an equally strong emerging American sentiment that the Irish and British governments, and the various parties on the ground, had to begin sorting out their differences without an American referee.

Although less engaged with Anglo–Irish affairs than his predecessor, George W. Bush has paid more attention to the matter than many expected. He has maintained an envoy to Northern Ireland, and continued the policy of treating the Irish and British governments with what might be called a parity of esteem.

Given the close, interlocking links between Britain, Ireland and the USA, there will probably always be something of an American dimension.

I began covering Ireland largely by default. By the mid-1980s the
conflict in Northern Ireland had settled into a long slog, and most American
correspondents based in London, with much of the continent their oyster,
seemed to spend as little time in Ireland as possible.

I persuaded my editors at *The Boston Globe* that covering Ireland for a
newspaper in a circulation area where roughly a third of the readers were of Irish
ancestry made it the one foreign story that was also a local story. A generous
colleague based in London gave his blessing, perhaps secretly relieved that he
wouldn't have to book into the Europa Hotel anymore. My editors let me travel
to Ireland several times each year, so I ended up spending more time on the
ground there than the London-based correspondents. Boston, meanwhile, got as
much traffic from the various parties in the North as Dublin and London, so there
was always something to write about at home.

I brought to the job a rudimentary understanding of Anglo–Irish relations, and
a breathtaking amount of naiveté. On one of my first reporting trips to Belfast,
I decided I needed to seek out the loyalist perspective. I drove around east
Belfast until I found a sufficiently large mural of King William of Orange painted
on the gable wall of a pub.

Inside the pub, the locals weren't especially friendly, eyeing me warily.
After a while, though, some conversation developed, and I introduced myself.
Gradually, I noticed the mostly elderly men who were at the bar melted away,
replaced by younger, harder men, all of whom seemed to have tattoos on their
forearms. 'What'd ye say ye name was?' one of the tattoos asked. 'Kevin, is it?'
I nodded. 'And where'd ye say ye was from?' he asked. 'Boston, is it?'

It suddenly dawned on me that this was not going well. I was now completely
surrounded by an imposing circle of young, seemingly hostile men. 'My
middle name is Billy,' I said. It was an odd, desperate gambit, made with little
forethought. The men surrounding me seemed to take a step back, as if I had
drawn a weapon. 'It is not,' one of the men, in the back, protested. It was then
that I thanked my lucky stars for the Italian lady who worked at the clerk's office

where my parents registered my birth in Boston. The woman stumbled over the middle name that my mother had handwritten on the application.

'It's Liam,' my mother told her.

'Lee-um? Lee-um?' the Italian lady said. 'What's a Lee-um?'

'It's Irish, for William,' my mother replied.

And so the Italian lady in the clerk's office entered my name as Kevin William Cullen, a fact unknown to me or anyone else in my family until, at the age of 12, I had to get a birth certificate to play little league baseball.

And so, all these years later, I'm sitting at the bar in this godforsaken loyalist pub in east Belfast, and these guys with tattooed forearms are passing my Massachusetts driver's license around the bar, demanding to see with their own eyes the oxymoronic teaming of what I learned was a Taig name and a Prod name. One of the tattoos was so kind as to step outside and tell a group of men to stop rocking my car, moments before it was to be tipped over.

I learned many things that day. One was that I was fortunate to have encountered the tattoos in the afternoon, before they were so inebriated that they would not have seen the humour in my hamfisted journey into the Loyalist heartland. And I never again used a rental car with southern plates while on assignment in Northern Ireland.

The tattoos told me they thought I was a member of Noraid, the American-based IRA support group, who came over on tours given by Republicans, and that I had come to wind them up on what would have amounted to a suicide mission. The tattoos seemed stunned to learn that I was an American journalist, genuinely wanting to get a Loyalist perspective.

Over the years, especially when interviewing Loyalist paramilitaries, that sort of inferiority complex constantly surfaced. Unionists of all stripes often complained that they were misunderstood, their grievances ignored by a press corps, especially American journalists, who were beguiled by the IRA and Republican revolutionaries.

My name and the location of my employer led many to assume I had Nationalist sympathies, and it was a constant battle to convince players on all sides that

I was striving to be fair and objective. My name, and the place where my newspaper is published, also led to other assumptions. In 1995, during the White House Conference on Northern Ireland, I joined a ludicrous scrum of journalists who were chasing Gerry Adams and Paddy Mayhew around the Sheraton Washington, trying to catch a glimpse of the first handshake between the Sinn Féin leader and Britain's Secretary of State.

Alas, it happened behind closed doors, and as Adams stepped out of a hotel room to brief us on the handshake, he prefaced his remarks, as was his wont, with a lengthy prologue in Irish. A group of English hacks turn to me, assuming that, with my pedigree, I spoke fluent Irish.
'What's he saying?' one of the English hacks whispered.
'He's saying, 'I think you're all a bunch of assholes. Could you please go home,' I whispered back.
The English hacks dutifully wrote down every word.

iii

There is no doubt that, since 1994, Adams and Sinn Féin have enjoyed a meteoric rise in popularity in the USA. Adams generally gets good press. He's impressive in broadcast interviews, and many US politicians have clamoured to be seen with him.

There has been much made of how much money Sinn Féin has raised in the USA. But the embrace of Adams and his party by the American mainstream was always conditional. It was based on the premise that Adams, Martin McGuinness and other Sinn Féin leaders had worked long and hard to convince physical force Republicans to step aside and let democratic politics become the engine that drives the movement.

In the American corridors of power and affluence, revolutionary chic only holds sway when those involved are former revolutionaries.

In the autumn of 2005, I was sitting in Ted Kennedy's private Senate respite on Capitol Hill, a lounge he calls The Hideaway. Kennedy, the liberal lion of the US Senate and the most influential Irish-American politician of his generation, fingered a chess set that is one of his prized possessions. The pieces are carved in the form of real-life figures who played a central role in the Troubles.

Some of the pieces are laden with poignant, even tragic symbolism. The pawns are RUC men and balaclava-clad Provos. Ian Paisley and Gerry Adams are knights, on opposing sides, of course. Some are more straightforwardly cast. Cahal Daly is a bishop, and the Queen is, well, a queen.

Listening to Kennedy talk about how much the political and cultural landscape had changed in Ireland over the past 35 years was to be transported on a tour de horizon of the Irish-American experience in the Troubles. At the height of the violence, in the early 1970s, Kennedy called for British withdrawal from Northern Ireland. As he became more familiar with the situation on the ground, Kennedy's words and actions became more nuanced. He championed John Hume's moderate Nationalism. He condemned violence from all sides: Republican, Loyalist and security forces. He lobbied for a political, negotiated settlement.

It was Kennedy who persuaded Bill Clinton to give Gerry Adams a visa in January 1994, convinced that it would pave the way to an IRA ceasefire, and show the benefits of entering the political mainstream. Employing the same reasoning, Kennedy snubbed Adams in the spring of 2005, in the wake of the murder of Belfast man Robert McCartney by an IRA that Kennedy called 'an albatross' around Sinn Féin's neck. Instead, Kennedy, a man whose two older brothers were assassinated, greeted McCartney's sister and fiancée. Even one of Sinn Féin's staunchest allies in Congress, US Representative Peter King of New York, went public, saying the IRA was hurting the party.

The insistence that the IRA go away was repeated by many other Americans, often in private, not wanting to embarrass Sinn Féin figures whom they had come to know and like. Within weeks of the St Patrick's Day debacle in Washington, Adams called on the IRA to end its armed campaign formally and to devote its attention and energy to politics. A few months later, the IRA said it would.

Sitting in his Hideway, between votes in the Senate, Ted Kennedy spoke sympathetically about poor Protestants in dreary housing estates such as

Glencairn in West Belfast, and lamented that the Loyalist parties had not been able to sustain the momentum of the 1990s. He spoke of how much he liked David Ervine, seeing him as a politician who could some day represent not just working-class Protestants, but Catholics, too. 'Ervine gets it,' Kennedy said. Ted Kennedy, sitting around the US Capitol, singing the praises of a Loyalist. It seemed ... historic.

In January 2006 John and Pat Hume visited Boston, ostensibly so that Hume could give the annual lecture at Boston University commemorating the birthday of one of his heroes, Martin Luther King Jr. A portrait of King dominated Hume's office in Derry throughout the Troubles.

But Hume's visit also marked something of an effort by the Social Democratic and Labour Party to raise its profile in the USA, to reclaim some of the territory it had lost to Sinn Féin in America over the past decade. Sitting in the Brookline home of his old friend Liz Shannon, widow of the former US Ambassador to Ireland, Hume said that many people tend to overlook the most fundamental American influence on modern Anglo–Irish relations: that the civil rights movement of blacks in the USA was the model for the civil rights movement of Catholic Nationalists in Northern Ireland. 'We believed in the words of Dr King,' Hume said. 'We believed that true unity among all people in Ireland had to be unity based on agreement, not just unity of the soil.' It wasn't the territory of Ireland that was divided, Hume said: it was the people, the two traditions, one Irish Nationalist, the other British Unionist:

'And Dr King taught us, you don't bring people together by killing them, or persecuting them, or discriminating against them. His dream called on the people of the United States to live up to the idealism of this country, something you find on a coin: *E Pluribus Unum*' – from many we are one. Those are the same words that inspired us to work for peace in Ireland.'

iv

In assessing the American dimension in Anglo–Irish relations, historians will inevitably devote most attention to politics and politicians, especially the way Bill Clinton replaced decades of Washington's laissez-faire policy toward

Northern Ireland with hands-on diplomacy, so that an American presided over the negotiations that led to the Good Friday Agreement. But I would argue the most important commodity Americans brought to the table was attitude, specifically the attitude that what was long thought of as impossible was, in fact, possible.

Who, 20 years ago, would have thought the Irish economy would become the Celtic Tiger? American businesses did, attracted by the available workforce and the Irish Republic's low corporate taxes. American confidence in the Irish economy, in turn, made Ireland not just more affluent, but more confident. That confidence was not limited to economic matters. The Irish approached their relationship with the British on a more equal footing. The British, meanwhile, saw not a former colony, but a partner, especially in the European Union. As the Republic became more affluent and secular, the old stereotype of it being a clerically dominated economic basket case – what a poet once called 'Albania with ceili music' – faded from view. American investment, infused with a can-do optimism, produced returns beyond the economic realm.

Throughout the Troubles, the conflict was often described as intractable. It was a description that many Irish and Britons subscribed to. But it was one that many Americans would not. Call it idealism, call it naiveté, but many Americans looked at Irish Nationalists and British Unionists and saw how much more they had in common than divided them. Perhaps because of distance, both physical and emotional; perhaps because they had seen in their own country how the Irish and British had seemed so alike compared with the other racial and ethnic groups that make up a vast, diverse nation, Americans saw as eminently resolvable a conflict that so many on the immediate fringes of it deemed as hopeless.

And while many in the opposing camps in Northern Ireland were busy insisting that outsiders could not possibly understand their grievances, Americans, more than most, suggested the conflict over power, history and national allegiances was in fact a universal one – that if the Salvadorans could end their civil war, that if the South Africans could end the dreadful era of apartheid without a conflagration, certainly people living in a place roughly the size of Connecticut could come to some peaceful accommodation.

In an effort to get those on the island of Ireland thinking more globally, Padraig O'Malley, an academic at the University of Massachusetts in Boston, did much to bring the various parties in Northern Ireland together with the black and white politicians who steered South Africa through the end of apartheid. In 1992, politicians from Northern Ireland and South Africa came together for the first time, in Boston. There were follow-up meetings in Boston, Belfast and South Africa.

The meetings were not without incident. O'Malley remembers that, at one gathering in South Africa, the DUP deputy leader, Peter Robinson, complained that the Shinners had better accommodation than the DUPers. When O'Malley asked how Robinson had arrived at such a conclusion, Robinson noted that the Sinn Féin rooms had mini-bars while the DUP ones did not:

'But Peter,' O'Malley protested, 'you people don't drink.'

'That's not the point,' Robinson replied.

Disputes over accommodation notwithstanding, the American-brokered meetings that brought the South Africans to the table did much to get people to look over the peace walls.

In early 2000, Sathyandranath Maharaj, known to his friends as Mac, returned to Johannesburg after failing to find a breakthrough in the impasse over the fate of IRA weapons. He met up with Cyril Ramaphosa, his comrade from the African National Congress, another old hand in the Byzantine world of Ulster politics. Mac Maharaj, one of Nelson Mandela's closest confidantes, and one of the last ANC fighters to lay down his arms, had gone to Belfast with the man who, in apartheid South Africa, had been his white counterpart: Leon Wessels, the cabinet minister in charge of security. Maharaj and Wessels tried to persuade the pols in Belfast that they were throwing away a golden opportunity, but the power-sharing government was suspended before it could collapse, at just 72 days old. All over the world, everybody said the peace process was on the brink of collapse. But Mac Maharaj had a different outlook. 'This,' he told Ramaphosa, 'is soluble.' The South Africans, like the Americans who got them involved in the first place, always had more faith in the politicians and the people in Northern Ireland than those people and politicians had in themselves. They had an irreverent optimism, and in any place where people are set in their ways, looking backward for guidance instead of forward, irreverence comes in handy.

v

I have a confession to make, and this is as good a place to make it as any. Some years ago, when the peace process was in full bloom and everything looked possible, an Irish woman whom I had known for many years came to me, seeking advice. She said she was conflicted: she had been invited to the British Consul General's house in Boston for a reception, because she was involved in a charity that also involved both the Irish and British governments.

What's the problem? I asked. Well, she is a Republican, from a staunch Republican family, and if her mammy back home in Ireland found out she had gone to the British consul's house, it'd just about kill the old woman. My American solution for an Anglo–Irish dilemma: steal an ashtray.
'What?' my friend asked.
'Go to the reception and steal an ashtray,' I said. 'It'll make you feel better.' And so she did, slipping it into her purse when no-one was looking. In the end, the Irish nuns, who had instilled in my friend a healthy sense of right and wrong, wielded more influence than American irreverence, and she put the ashtray back before she left the reception.

But, she had to admit, while it rested there, hidden in her purse, it sure felt good.

Marianne Elliott

Professor Marianne Elliott is Director of the Institute of Irish Studies at Liverpool University. She was born in Belfast, and is internationally recognised as one of Ireland's leading historians, best known for her acclaimed biography Wolfe Tone: Prophet of Irish Independence, *which won numerous awards. Her other books include* Partners in Revolution: The United Irishmen and France; Robert Emmet: The Making of a Legend; *and* The Catholics of Ulster: A History. *In 2005 she was invited to deliver the prestigious Ford Lectures at Oxford University on 'Religion and Identity in Irish History'. Professor Elliott served on the Opsahl Commission in 1993, co-writing its report, 'A Citizens' Inquiry'. Her research interests are political and cultural history, religious identities, eighteenth-century Ireland and France, and the history of Ulster. In October 2000 she was awarded an OBE for services to Irish Studies and the Northern Ireland peace process, and in 2002 she was elected a Fellow of the British Academy.*

Hyphenated hybrids: Irishness, Englishness and religious identities in Britain and Ireland
Marianne Elliott

One of William Carleton's funniest stories, *Phil Purcell, The Pig Driver*, portrays the Irish pig as a species superior to the English pig. The latter, as a result of having been shut up in sties, had become soft, but the free-roaming, liberty-loving Irish pig was altogether smarter and fitter. Accordingly, when Phil drove his Irish pigs to market in England, they escaped the sties and fed well on the neat English country gardens. With one pig left to sell before his return to Ireland, Phil assumed the guise of Phadhrumshagh Corfuffle, a migrant Irish labourer, using the English gentry's condescending perceptions of him as a specimen Irish simpleton to sell the same pig many times over. They were even impressed at his ingeniously economical feeding strategy: a rota of feeding and starving the pig on alternate days, thereby alternating the fat and the lean to ensure perfect streaky bacon. But while Phil had paraded himself as something of an Irish spailpín or migrant harvest labourer, he had in fact 'made it' in Britain, and duly brought the proceeds of his success home.

Here we have some of the many contradictory stereotypes that have fed into our neighbouring national identities. Sigmund Freud, after all, applied his 'narcissism of minor differences' to space and territory: 'it is precisely communities with adjoining territories, and related to each other in their ways as well, who are engaged in constant feuds and in ridiculing each other'[1] Meanwhile, let us note that when most Irish people use the term British, they really mean English, and the use of the term by the Scots and Welsh, let alone by northern Protestants, is a constant puzzle (not least to second- and third-generation Irish in England). In this essay I want to look at the stereotypes that have historically informed Irish and English perceptions of one other. They are fast disappearing. But given the ease with which extreme nationalists in Ireland can still play on the '800-years-of-English-oppression' reading of Irish history (it was, after all, still taught in Irish school textbooks until the 1960s), politely sweeping them under the carpet is ill-advised.

i

The Irish craftiness and English condescension invoked by the story of Phil Purcell are timeless stereotypes. Beware their wiles more than their wars, warned the twelfth-century Giraldus Cambrensis, whose *Topography of Ireland* inspired a trend in English writings about Ireland through many centuries, and equally provoked Irish rebuttals in the form of 'the island of saints and scholars' counter-myth. This is pre-eminently and most influentially expounded in Geoffrey Keating's 1634 *History of Ireland*: 'Every one of the new *Galls* (the English) who writes on Ireland writes ... in imitation of Cambrensis ... who is the bull of the herd for them writing the false history of Ireland'.[2] Although often quite complimentary, Giraldus's message is that their love of freedom has made the Irish libertines lazy and deceitful. It starts at birth when, contrary to English practice, nature is left to take its course and Irish infants are not swaddled, nor is frequent hot water used to lengthen their limbs, raise their noses, or press down their faces. They prefer wandering, 'primitive', pastoral ways, which he thinks makes them lazy and lacking in ambition, and all of this is reflected in their 'barbarous' loose dress and long hair.

Herein we have the standard English stereotype of the Irish which, after the Reformation, was transferred to the Irish Catholics, not least by Edmund Spenser. Indeed, although the Elizabethan period witnessed a more modern and sceptical writing of history generally, Tudor writers were prepared to believe just about anything portraying Ireland's barbarity, so influential had Cambrensis been.[3] Spenser set the agenda when he argued that the Irish were inherently barbarous and it was England's historic mission to establish civility and true religion through conquest. He continued Canbrensis's attack on Irish people's manner of living in 'boolies' (their transhumance needs requiring mobile, impermanent homes), their thick hair and mantles, their lurking (there is a lot of 'lurking' in Spenser) in glens and fastnesses, their homes 'rather swine-styes than houses ... a beastly manner of life ... living together with his beast in one house'.[4] By depicting the Irish pig's proximity to humans as one of the reasons for his superior intelligence, Carleton's satire deftly turns the tables on this. The very shape of the landscape, with its prevalent bogland and forests, was attributed to national indolence. Draining, clearing, taming and building became part of the Protestant civilising mission to Ireland. Stone buildings came to represent the perceived superiority of Protestant or English culture, and in modern times were still viewed as alien by the Irish and 'left to vanish unlamented'.[5]

Such has been the longevity of this stereotype that, when romanticism made the wildness of Ireland fashionable, English travellers were surprised to find there was more to Ireland than bogland.[6] 'Go back to the bogs where you came from', was the angry retort of the man in Chester, in his otherwise justified complaint at my lamentable car-parking. It still appears regularly in the colourful language of the Rev. Ian Paisley, and is caught in the 1970s poem by Patrick Williams, 'Cage under siege':

> On our borders the known world ends sheer.
> We've pulled the sea around us like a shawl
> And heaved the mountains higher. The waiting
> South's bog-barbarians starve against a grand
> Squiggle on our map.[7]

The self-identification of the 'Englishry' in Ireland continued this stand-offishness over many centuries. The arrival of the Anglo-Normans in the twelfth century was denounced by later Irish nationalists as the beginning of English rule in Ireland. But Gaelic Ireland scarcely registered it. Contemporary sources reflected confusion about the ethnicity of the newcomers. Initially, they were deemed 'French' or 'Franks', and later 'Saxain' (to denote English or English by blood) and 'Gaill', or foreigners residing in Ireland and generally understanding its language and culture, like the long-settled Hiberno-Norse. They could even be called 'Celts', because of the Bretons among them, or with even more justification 'Cambro-Normans', because of the large numbers of Welsh archers involved (making Walsh the most common non-Gaelic surname in Ireland). A variety of languages was spoken in Ireland during the middle ages, French remaining the official language until the fifteenth century. As late as 1541 a proclamation in English had to be translated into Irish for the Anglo-Irish peers attending parliament.[8]

However, there is still disagreement about what they called themselves, and in view of the determination of the long-settled and Catholic Anglo-Irish to lay claim to the term 'Old English' in the seventeenth century, it seems likely that they simply called themselves 'English'.[9] Catholicism was not yet a common bond with the 'Old Irish'. But in the late sixteenth and seventeenth centuries, the most recent, so-called 'New' English arrivals were aggressively promoting the idea that subjects could not be loyal if not they did not share the same religion as the ruler. After Cromwell they used the terms 'papist' and 'Irishman' interchangeably. The association of Catholicism and Irishness became, and has remained, one of the most durable of stereotypes, bedevilling diaspora studies, much as it has done other attempts to understand Ireland's past.

Given that there was confusion too about what to call the people actually inhabiting the area called England, historians came up with an unsatisfactory distinction: Anglo-Normans before 1216 and Anglo-Irish thereafter, although the latter does not appear in the records until the late fourteenth century and was not in general use until the late nineteenth century. These descendants of the twelfth-century Anglo-Normans were perceived as 'a 'middle nation' ... neither wholly English, nor yet Irish, but something 'in between'.[10] The hyphenated hybrid was to have a long and troubled pedigree. Many Irish Protestant writers came to criticise the fatalistic tendency of their coreligionists in accepting the definition Anglo-Irish, with all its propertied, upper-class and English associations. They had no doubt of their Irishness and were irritated at the tendency to see Protestant destinies through the image of Yeatsian decline and extinction. 'We are far more Irish than all the saints and martyrs – Parnell – Pearse – Madame Markievicz – Maud Gonne – de Valera', Lily Yeats chastised her brother W.B. Yeats, 'and no one ever thinks of speaking of them as Anglo-Irish.'[11]

In the classic statement of Irish Protestant nationalism in 1697, William Molyneux countered the claims of the British Parliament to legislate for Ireland by denying Britain's assumed rights through conquest. Since 'the great body of the present People of Ireland are the Progeny of the English and Britains, that from time to time have come over into this Kingdom; and there remains but a meer handful of the Antient Irish', the various contests were not like wars between foreign enemies giving the victor right of conquest. Rather, they were 'Rebellions, or *Intestine Commotions* ... the *Irish Papists* rising against the *King and Protestants of Ireland*.'[12] The Protestant nation, in other words, was no subject people, much as England tended to treat them that way. Of course, later commentators would point out the fallacy of this small Protestant elite's claim to be the Irish nation, to the exclusion of Catholics and Dissenters. But the discordance was not noted at the time, and these Protestant patriots were particularly incensed at England's tendency to conflate them with the 'savage Irish', in the words of Jonathan Swift, writing in 1724.[13]

In a very witty autobiographical sketch of his Irish upbringing by the doyen of 'imagined' national identity, Benedict Anderson explains the dilemma of the Irish Protestant, somehow caught in between Irishness and Britishness. Although his family was Irish on his father's side and his childhood was spent in Waterford, neither he nor his parents had actually been born in Ireland. As proof of Irish ancestry was required for an Irish passport, his search took him down two stereotypical routes, one Gaelic/Catholic-Irish, one Anglo/Protestant-Irish. In his anthropological research, he was quite accustomed to the concept of selective ancestry. But his search for the height of Irish national purity – the anti-English, rebel, Catholic Gael – was to prove just how selective that definition of Irishness actually is. He found enough ancestors to fit the stereotype of the Catholic Gael – some rebels, exiles, Catholic or nationalist campaigners – to give a veneer of Gaelic respectability. But he also found 'mixed marriages' and Gaels who anglicised their names, became English officials and soldiers and, even in exile, remained steadfastly elitist – not much sign here of the poor downtrodden Gael of the Irish Catholic identikit.[14]

The reason that Anderson's ancestors did not fit the identikit – indeed why most Irish do not – is because it has been fine-tuned by propagandists over centuries. It is why Irish Protestants came to be dismissed as 'England's faithful garrison', according to Sean Lemass in 1927. It lies at the heart of the confused identities in Northern Ireland, with Protestants often perceived as blow-ins and planters, creating fears of how they might be treated in a predominantly Catholic Ireland. Thus the confusion in Irish nationalism, or sectors of it: was it the English or the Protestants it wanted rid of? – an ambivalence noted by generations of nervous Irish Protestants.

ii

Yet how anti-English *were* the Irish Catholics? They had, after all, created a new Gaelic pedigree for the Protestant James I on his accession to the throne in

1603, and remained loyal to the Stuarts thereafter. As eighteenth-century
Catholic leaders liked to point out, they were on the side of the legitimate
monarchs in both 1641 and 1690; they supported Britain in the American War of
Independence (unlike the Presbyterians), and spent much of the penal era trying
to show that Catholics could be loyal to a Protestant state. Catholics' traditional
loyalty to the person of the monarch revived with the Hanoverians after 1714,
with the recognition that religious tolerance existed in Hanover, and is present
in the oaths of the seditious Catholic Defenders (a presence that baffled
generations of Irish commentators, nurtured on the anti-Englishness of later
nationalism). Catholics had been given little reason to trust the Irish Protestants.
England had been a far better friend to them, and independence held no
advantage. Indeed Wolfe Tone suspected that, once Catholic emancipation
was granted, Irish Catholics would be happy with the British connection.

Catholics under the penal laws came to depend on England overruling the
extreme Protestantism of the Irish Parliament. Every Catholic relief act in the
eighteenth century was initiated by England – a trend that came to an abrupt
end in the 1790s but was not made publicly apparent until after the Act of
Union in 1800, when George III's personal hostility to Catholic emancipation
became known. The sectarianism of the Irish Parliament – with its predominantly
landed element – had always been greater than that in the country at large, and
they frequently played on the landed class's fears of losing land acquired in the
previous century in order to deter moderation. Yet, out in the country, the notion
of land justly acquired was important to the landed classes, and it was far less
easy to dispossess Catholics than has commonly been supposed. By then,
England had more contempt for the Irish Protestant Ascendancy than the Irish
Catholics. Loss of confidence in the Ascendancy's ability to rule Ireland was
a significant factor in the decision to abolish the Irish Parliament with the Act
of Union.

Now, all Irish people were British citizens, although whether the British identity
could ever really be sufficiently separated from Englishness to accommodate
other national identities remains an issue, even today.[15] Suffice it to say that the
strange status of Ireland *vis-à-vis* England – not quite 'conquered', not quite
a 'colony', not quite fully assimilated into the UK – continued to be reflected
even after Irish independence. Until 1948, Irish people were still entitled to

British citizenship, and today the Irish are the only non-British group entitled to enter without passports and have the same rights as British-born to social services and to vote in elections. This makes the 'passive victim'[16] reading of Irish migration to England overly simplistic. Much of it is based on assumptions about anti-Irishness in England, which are not necessarily valid. I listened recently to a successful middle-class Londoner tell of his family's bitterness at anti-Irishness encountered in the 1950s, and it reminded me of the west Belfast nationalist described by Dervla Murphy in by far the best book ever to be written on the Troubles in Northern Ireland: *A Place Apart*.

> 'It was ... impossible to unhook Gerry from the past [which to him was one of constant oppression]; he seemed to need his grievance, to have built his whole personality around it ... so much resentment – generations of resentment, forming the very marrow of his soul.'[17]

I have frequently encountered similar resentment among second-generation Irish in England. And yet they are usually very successful people, often having risen through an educational system that would not have been available to them had their parents remained in Ireland. Again, the analogy with Catholics in Northern Ireland is not inappropriate: a victim-reading of the past enhancing every hint of anti-Irishness or anti-Catholicism encountered in the present.

iii

After the Union, Irish people arrived in Britain in increasing numbers – particularly once cheaper travel was introduced in the 1820s. Stereotypical anti-Irishness was encountered more in Scotland than in England, and more in the north-west of England than elsewhere. Contrary to the stereotype, the Irish in Britain did not languish in labouring and unskilled trades, and whatever the prejudice of thinkers such as Carlyle and Macaulay, they were valued by employers, supplying shortages created by the industrial revolution in the nineteenth century, much as gaps created by wartime service in the Second World War created opportunities for some 100 000 Irish people between 1939 and 1945. Remittances back to Ireland between 1939 and 1969 have been calculated in billions of pounds.[18]

By the late nineteenth century, the Irish emigrant to England was as likely to be aspiring middle class, attending public schools in England (not least the Catholic ones), and servicing the expanding British Empire. Alike with Young Irelander William Smith O'Brien, you could denounce English misrule of Ireland, yet welcome the empire as mediating a new kind of identity.[19] This process was being satirised in *The Nation* newspaper as early as 1843:

> 'Mrs. O'Rourke to her sister Debby in England, Ballsassenagh
> *[A play on the Irish word sasenach, a derogatory term for the English]*:
> I write, my dear Deb., in the greatest distress –
> How great it must be you will easily guess,
> When I tell you I am just about bidding adieu
> To poor Johnny and Jemmy. I'm sending the two
> To England to school. Oh! Debby, my heart
> Is ready to break, when I think I must part
> My dear darling boys; but it's all for their good,
> And I'd go through a thousand times more, if I could,
> To rear them *genteelly* – for ev'ry sensation
> Of mine is in favor of *nice* education.
> Above all, 'tis the accent I'm anxious about;
> Good accent's the main point beyond any doubt.
>
> I like a young man with an air supercilious,
> Looking English, and aristocratic, and bilious –
> It shows folk at once he has rank on his side,
> When he looks down on all with a cool, conscious pride.
>
> See the Blacks and the Browns – oh! it sorely annoys
> To see those young fellows look down on our boys;
> And why? I'm convinced it's for no better reason,
> Than that they were at college in England last season.'[20]

More prevalent among parents of the young going to England, however, have been fears that they will succumb either to its fleshpots or its footpads. And such fears pervaded all classes. An additional fear – from at least the second half of the nineteenth century – was that of losing their Catholicism in 'Protestant

England'. Emigration was deemed unpatriotic by the Irish Catholic clergy, and returning emigrants, flaunting their success, appeared as 'the recruiting sergeants of England' in Canon Sheehan's hugely popular novels.[21]

In the nineteenth century, Britain was unusual in Europe, having the largest number of Catholic subjects (mostly Irish) in an officially Protestant country. By mid-century four-fifths of Catholics in England were Irish. Although the London Government had sought Catholic emancipation since the early 1790s, the attempt to pass it in the British Parliament was blocked by popular anti-Catholicism. English Catholics had followed a quietist, assimilationist policy in the past, and the gulf between them and the poorer Irish Catholics pouring into England remained well into the next century. Indeed, had Catholic emancipation been purely for English Catholics, it almost certainly would have come sooner. As further reforms started to dismantle the Protestant state, Britain presented the contradictory image of being at once the most popularly anti-Catholic, yet most religiously liberal, state in Europe.[22]

However, Catholic emancipation came too late to endear Britain to Irish Catholics. The rise of romantic nationalism coincided with the 'devotional revolution' in the Irish Catholic Church, which was stamped with the anti-Englishness and anti-Protestantism of Cardinal Cullen. It was already there as a sub-current, particularly in the Irish-language poetry and song of the late seventeenth and eighteenth centuries – much of which was being made more widely available in the nineteenth century through translation into English. By the seventeenth century, Irish-language poems, often written by Catholic clerics, identified Catholicism with Irishness and spirituality; Protestantism with Englishness, foreignness and materialism. Ironically, it was the translation of these poems into English in the nineteenth century that assisted the further Catholicising of national identity during the campaign for Catholic emancipation. Among subscribers to the bilingual printed versions of the 1850s were all four Catholic archbishops of Ireland and 27 other Catholic bishops.[23]

Irish Catholicism was deemed peculiarly spiritual, because it wasn't English. By the late nineteenth century it was the materialism and ungodliness of Protestant England that became the theme of countless Catholic sermons and publications. To Irish minds, Englishness and Catholicism seemed contradictions.

Prayers for the conversion of England were a regular feature of Catholic worship from at least the 1830s. In Ireland, the 1929 centenary of Catholic emancipation took particular pleasure in reporting celebrations in the towns of 'Protestant England', but largely missed its significance for *English* Catholics, in what was treated overwhelmingly as an Irish issue. England was considered a missionary frontier, and the welfare of Irish Catholics going there (as much as those 'tripper-emigrants' bringing bad habits back) became a matter for national concern.

English Catholics were not deemed to be the real thing. Although, in the 1850s, there were more fundamental issues underlying John Henry Newman's disputes with the Irish bishops in his role as rector of the new Catholic University in Dublin, they were rather scandalised by his introduction of English ways and English staff.[24] The dangers of 'slippage', 'leakage' from the faith among Irish emigrants to England, is a frequent topic in Catholic journals. A series in *The Furrow* in the 1950s thought those Catholics going to England often regarded it as 'a vacation from religious practice'. If they came back to Ireland they might bring with them the easier ways of English Catholicism. 'Such things as Evening Service – the very name itself is suspect', 'more suggestive of a concert than a religious service'; and with the attempts to introduce the liturgy in English, English Catholicism was surely too close to High Anglicanism. All of which would 'give our average Irish Catholic the feeling that he had found in England a none-too-orthodox brand of Catholicism.'[25]

But if he stayed, the prognosis was worse. He might assimilate and become 'as English as the English themselves. Beer at the local, Sunday morning *News of the World*', the dominant culture having become 'cannibalistic of the other'. So assimilation was not to be encouraged. Irish parish priests should inform their opposite numbers in England of parishioners moving there; specific Irish leisure activities should be arranged; and the Irish-founded Legion of Mary set up stalls at Euston and Paddington stations to meet the boat-trains from Ireland. There can be no doubt that many Irish coming to work in England have welcomed the Church's help. However, it also contributed to the ghetto mentality of the Irish community in England and further reinforced the association of Irishness with Catholicism.

Much of this was a form of cultural defensiveness. Secure identities – personal and national – tend to be low-key. Sociologist Fr Michael MacGréil applied a 'patriotic esteem scale' in his attitude survey of the mid-1990s, and concluded that there was in Ireland 'a xenophobic sense of superiority *vis-à-vis* other nationalities and cultures' – high percentages of people believing Ireland better than most other countries, expressing pride in Irish history and defending Irish customs. 'The national respect ... verges on the ethnocentric. It could be interpreted as indicating a quasi-superiority complex, which may be a reaction to being so long kept under the thumb of their colonial master.'[26] 'Pagan England' was compared with 'holy Ireland'. The Gaelic revival's distaste for the great works of English literature, which had so alienated Joyce, and continued to inform censorship in independent Ireland, was in many ways a reaction against the assumed cultural inferiority of things Irish in the past. 'Let us drop for ever the idea that culture is the appendage of the Saxon and the Protestant', proclaimed the Dominican priest the Rev. A. M. Crofts in June 1929, in a public lecture about 'English misrule in Ireland'.[27] And much like the proverbial Joneses, independent Ireland was ever sensitive to criticism from the former ruler. It was, for example, embarrassment about hostile English press criticism of child abuse in Irish religious establishments that, more than anything else, produced reform.[28]

iv

This *Lives Entwined* project is taking place at a time of unprecedented good relations between England and Ireland, brought about not only by the ending of the Troubles in Northern Ireland, but by Ireland's new-found confidence and ability to deal with London as an equal. Gone is the old belief that Protestants cannot be Irish, while in England it is now fashionable to be Irish, second- and third-generation Irish in their teens and twenties displaying none of the sensitivities of those in their fifties and older. However, there is a tendency to ignore the sectarian Irishness that was, in itself, a response to English Protestantism's sense of cultural superiority. Nor does Ireland like to be reminded about the casualties who still relate to that older defensive identity, like the second-generation Irish from England with English accents, or the northern nationalists sounding no different from Ulster Prods. Yet it was often the anti-Catholicism of England and Britain that was mistaken for anti-Irishness in the past, and today the extraordinary media spying on Tony Blair's presumed

Rome-ward trend suggests a continuing vitality, much as does the reinvention of anti-Englishness and anti-Protestantism in Ireland as post-traumatic stress-speak or presumption that guilt should attach to future generations.[29]

In October 2000, I was being interviewed by a journalist from a reputable Irish newspaper. I have no recollection what triggered it, but I remember in vivid detail how irrelevant I quickly became as the journalist launched into an attack on Britain's role in the Great Famine. Tony Blair had just apologised for Britain's mishandling of that human disaster, but this was considered insufficient by the journalist. For the wrongs England had done to Ireland, compensation was needed. At this point I was reminded of the members of the Catholic Committee in the 1790s, who countered the accusation that their campaign for political rights was a ruse to take back confiscated land with the question: where would you start? – since their wealth and property also would have been in dispute.

And this is the point: whatever the antagonisms, the lives of past peoples in Ireland and Britain have been so intertwined that the pure Gael and the pure Anglo-Saxon do not exist, whatever their names and recent ancestry. It is impossible to understand the complexity of the relationship between the two countries without taking account of the fundamental equation between national and religious identity. The Troubles in Northern Ireland were part of its legacy and, while the growing secularisation of Britain and Ireland has contributed to the thaw in old antagonisms, a reminder that those antagonisms are still playing out in the North might recall to both powers that they, too, bear some responsibility for the conflict.

Endnotes

[1] Cited by Blok, Anton (1998) The narcissism of minor differences. *European Journal of Social Theory* i: 35.

[2] Gerald of Wales (Giraldus Cambrensis) (1988) *The History and Topography of Ireland*, trans. John O'Meara. Harmondsworth, UK: Penguin, p. 13; Keating, Geoffrey (1902) *Foras Feasa ar Éirinn, The History of Ireland* Vol. 1. Irish Texts Society, p. 153.

[3] Hadfield, Andrew (1993) Briton and Scythian: Tudor representations of Irish origins. *Irish Historical Studies* xxviii: 390–408.

[4] Spenser, Edmund (1809) A view of the State of Ireland. In: Ware, James (ed.) *Ancient Irish Histories* i. Dublin: Hibernia, p. 135.

[5] Barnard, T. C. (1993) The political, material and mental culture of the Cork settlers, c. 1650–1700. In: O'Flanagan, Patrick and Buttimer, Cornelius G., eds. *Cork. History and Society*. Dublin: Geography Publications, p. 310.

[6] Bowden, Charles Topham (1791) *A Tour through Ireland*. Dublin: W. Corbet, p. 218.

[7] Cited by Brown, Terence (1985) *The Whole Protestant Community: The Making of a Historical Myth*. Field Day, Pamphlet No 7., p. 9.

[8] Dolan, Terence (ed.) (1991) The literature of Norman Ireland. In: Deane, Seamus (ed.) *The Field Day Anthology of Irish Writing* i. Field Day, p. 143.

[9] Ellis, Steven (1996) Nationalist historiography and the English and Gaelic worlds. *Irish Historical Studies* xxv: 1–18.

[10] Cosgrave, Art (ed.) (1987) *A New History of Ireland, ii, Medieval Ireland 1169–1534*. Oxford: Oxford University Press, p. ixi.

[11] Cited by Foster, R. F. (1993) *Paddy and Mr Punch. Connections in Irish and English History.* Harmondsworth, UK: Allen Lane/Penguin, p. 296.

[12] Molyneux, William (1687) *The Case of Ireland Stated.* 1977 edn. Dublin: Cadenas Press, pp. 112–113.

[13] Swift, Jonathan (1724) The Drapier's Letters. In: Scott, T (ed.) (1903) *The Prose Works of Jonathan Swift,* D.D. Vol. vi. London: Chiswick Press.

[14] Anderson, Benedict (2003) Selective kinship. *The Dublin Review* Spring: 5–29 (my thanks to Roy Foster for drawing this to my attention.)

[15] Howe, Steven (2000) *Ireland and Empire. Colonial Legacies in Irish History and Culture.* Oxford: Oxford University Press, p. 41 (for a good survey of the problem).

[16] Akenson, D. H. (1997) *If the Irish ran the World: Montserrat, 1630–1730.* Liverpool: Liverpool University Press, p. 175. (Don Akenson – undoubtedly the most acclaimed historian of the Irish diaspora – argues repeatedly that this notion of emigration as 'exile' and of the Irish experience of emigration as exceptional, is quite unhistorical.)

[17] Murphy, Dervla (1978) *A Place Apart.* London: Penguin, p. 203.

[18] Akenson, D. H. (2005) *An Irish History of Civilisation* Vol. ii. Montreal and Kingston: McGill and Queen's University Press, pp. 536–537; MacRaild, Donald M. (1999) *Irish Migrants in Modern Britain,* 1750–1922. London: Macmillan, pp. 51–53.

[19] Ridden, Jennifer (2004) Britishness as an imperial and diasporic identity: Irish elite perspectives, c. 1820–70s. In: Gray, Peter (ed.) *Victoria's Ireland. Irishness and Britishness 1837–1991.* Dublin: Four Counts Press, p. 88. (Between 1815 and 1910 about a third of white settlers in the British empire were Irish.)

[20] Anon (1843) English schools and Irish pupils. *The Nation,* 8 April.

[21] Cited by Candy, Catherine (1995) *Priestly Fictions.* Dublin: Wolfhound Press, p. 91.

22 Atkin, Nicholas and Tallet, Frank (2003) *Priests, Prelates and People. A History of European Catholicism since 1750*. London: I.B. Tauris, pp. 95–98.

23 My thanks to Vincent Morley for making available to me his unpublished paper 'Views of the past in Irish vernacular literature, 1650–1850'.

24 Norman, E. R. (1984) *The English Catholic Church in the Nineteenth Century*. Oxford: Oxford University Press, pp. 323–324.

25 Culhane, Robert (1950) Irish Catholics in Britain. *The Furrow* i: 387–388.

26 MacGréil, Micheál (1996) *Prejudice in Ireland Revisited*. Maynooth: St Patrick's College, pp. 102–103; Twomey, D. Vincent (2003) *The End of Irish Catholicism?* Dublin: Veritas Publications, p. 30.

27 Anon (1929) The darkest days of Irish history. Laws that failed to crush the Ancient Faith. *The Irish Independent*, 21 June.

28 Ferriter, Diarmaid (2004) *The Transformation of Ireland* 1900–2000. London: Profile Books, pp. 588–589.

29 See, for example, the front-page *Sunday Times* report, 2 April 2006, by Christopher Morgan: 'Franciscan friar holds masses for Blairs in No 10', replete with wafers, secretiveness and shifty monks – it could have appeared in the 'scarlet whore'-like sermons of any number of fundamentalist evangelical Protestants down to, and including, the Rev. Ian Paisley.

Ed Moloney

Ed Moloney began writing about the Troubles in Northern Ireland in 1978, when he was asked to contribute pieces to Magill *magazine, thus beginning a long, productive and always turbulent relationship with Vincent Browne. He then worked for a year at* Hibernia *magazine before joining* The Irish Times, *initially in Dublin but then in the Belfast office, where he was eventually made Northern Editor. He and* The Irish Times *parted company on the eve of the Anglo–Irish Agreement in 1985, after which he co-authored the unauthorised biography,* Paisley. *He then teamed up for several more bumpy years with Vincent Browne, who had started* The Sunday Tribune, *survived both his tenure and departure, but then fell badly foul of one of Browne's many successors. In 2001, while finishing his study of Gerry Adams's stewardship of the IRA and the peace process,* A Secret History of the IRA, *he moved to New York with his wife where, a few weeks after the book was serialised in the* Tribune, *he learned he had been sacked from the paper. He has no regrets leaving Ireland.*

The peace process and journalism
Ed Moloney

Introduction

I remember the moment, as vividly as if it had happened yesterday, when it became clear to me that the peace process had led us all into a journalistic wilderness. Not long after the Good Friday Agreement was signed in 1998, a BBC Radio 4 producer asked me to take part in a debate framed around the following question: 'If you, as a journalist, discovered information that was damaging to the peace process, would you go ahead and publish it?'

Alongside me that day, in a tiny studio in the BBC's Ormeau Avenue headquarters in Belfast, sat veteran Downtown Radio reporter Eamonn Mallie. By that stage in his professional life, Mallie had carved out a name as one of Ireland's best radio journalists and was regaled as a 'media character', famous for his persistently tough questioning at press conferences, no matter how high or mighty the person on the receiving end. He was from Crossmaglen in the heart of South Armagh's notorious 'bandit country', where the IRA's writ had run more-or-less unhampered for two decades or so. Despite his roots, Mallie was no Provo-loving reporter, and had given Sinn Féin and the IRA as hard a time as any reporter, especially on the many occasions when they deserved it. In fact, like the best pros, he had cultivated sources from every political quarter in Northern Ireland and, in one of the most unlikely liaisons of the Troubles, had even managed to strike up a relationship with Ian Paisley. It paid off. His sources inside the Democratic Unionist Party helped him to break one of the best stories of the peace process, the revelation that the British Government had been talking secretly to the IRA leadership.

He treated the DUP and the IRA in the same indiscriminate way, as potentially rich veins of journalistic gold, otherwise known as stories. But much like myself, Mallie also strongly believed that the IRA had to be treated seriously by journalists for a very basic and important reason: understanding the seemingly endless Troubles of Northern Ireland would be impossible without trying to explain why, after more than 20 years of warfare, the IRA and Sinn Féin were still very much around. At a time when journalists of such stripe were thin on the ground, it was always reassuring to see Mallie join the pack of reporters covering a story.

That day in the BBC however, to my great surprise and disappointment, I found myself completely at odds with Eamonn. He would kill a story rather than harm the peace process; I would not.

My view was simple. To paraphrase Mrs Thatcher on an entirely different subject, a story was a story was a story, and there was no way I could or would allow consequences for the peace process or anything else to get in the way. I believed then, and still do, that a journalist's obligation to report or broadcast a story overrides every other consideration, with only one exception: if putting a story into the public domain could directly lead to loss of life or injury, then it should be set aside for another day. Otherwise my rule was straightforward: publish and be damned. Besides, if the peace process was strongly rooted, it would survive even the most damaging story; if it wasn't then it would probably fail – and deserve to fail – from some other cause anyway.

Eamonn differed sharply, and ventured that securing peace and ending the Troubles came before everything, even the most enticing story. I was bewildered and a dozen questions rushed to my lips. Was I really hearing this? Wasn't this breaking the cardinal rule of journalism, that reporters should never pick sides in a story or make value judgements, no matter what their private views? What was the point in being a reporter if you covered up the truth or misled people, either deliberately or otherwise? If you believed this, should you level with your editor, your readers or listeners? Or should you keep it a secret from them? And if you did tell them, could anything you wrote or broadcast be believed? If you didn't, how could you face yourself in the mirror each morning? One question I held back: had Eamonn already crossed this Rubicon and spiked stories that he believed would cause problems for the peace process?

If I single out Eamonn Mallie in this regard, it is not because he was the only journalist in Belfast to hold such views, nor the most forceful in expressing them, but because my experience in the BBC that day with him was both traumatic and a harbinger of things to come. The truth is that many of my colleagues agreed with Eamonn; the debate between us and the disagreement that quickly surfaced was but a foretaste of what would become, as the peace process gathered pace, a sadly unwelcome but increasingly common journalistic phenomenon.

i

If the reportage of the peace process can be characterised by any particular quality, it was the willingness of too many journalists not to ask the hard questions that ought to have been asked. The peace process heralded an extraordinary, but deeply puzzling and confusing transition in Northern Ireland's troubled history and it was vital that journalists should have attempted to explain all this as best they could. Never was there a time in Northern Ireland's painful and bloody history when information was more necessary or potentially socially useful. But in practice many reporters shrank from doing their jobs, and were – and still are – content to be mere stenographers of the peace process for fear that they could be accused, at the very least, of being 'unhelpful' to the process, and at worst, of being actively opposed to it.

In an important sense, this was the logical outworking of 30 years of 'Troubles' journalism, during which reporters and editors were intimidated by censorship laws or succumbed to the most insidious and enfeebling media ailment of all, self-censorship. In the Republic of Ireland, official media censorship was enshrined in Section 31 of the Broadcasting Act, which was introduced at the very outset of the Troubles in 1971 and refined in 1976. It gave the Government sweeping powers to ban anything from the airwaves that it considered sympathetic to political violence, and excluded specific organisations from radio and television, including the IRA and its political wing Sinn Féin. Section 31 applied legally only to the electronic media, not to the print media, but in practice its influence was all-embracing. Government support for Section 31 arose out of an atmosphere that was almost hysterical in its fear of the IRA and dread that the Northern Troubles would spill violently onto the streets of Dublin and other towns in the South, threatening not just the citizens of the Republic, but the stability and institutions of the state. In practice the impulse to censor was felt in all sections of the Irish media.

It is no exaggeration to say that the South experienced its own version of McCarthyism in those days. Just as the American media were trawled for Communist supporters in the early 1950s, so in the 1970s Irish journalists, in newspapers as well as in radio and TV, were scrutinised for IRA or Republican sympathies. Terms like 'fellow-traveller' and 'sneaking-regarder' entered the lexicon of Irish journalism. Irish journalists learned that the worst way to advance career prospects was by showing an interest in the North, or writing stories that could be construed as helpful – that word again – to the IRA. Conversely, the best way to get ahead was to trumpet anti-republicanism as loudly and widely as possible.

When I got my first full-time job in Irish journalism in 1979, as a Northern correspondent for the now defunct weekly review *Hibernia*, the Birmingham Six, Maguire Seven and Guildford Four, all alleged IRA bombers caught in England, had spent about 4 years in jail, and evidence was beginning to emerge casting doubt on their guilt. Eventually all three cases collapsed and the 17 men and women were completely exonerated in an episode that has entered the record books as one of the worst miscarriages of justice in British judicial history.

But outside the columns of *Hibernia* there was virtually no sign of any media interest, either broadcast or print, in any of these stories in the Ireland of 1979, and the reason was not difficult to fathom. Anyone questioning the guilt of these alleged IRA members was implicitly doubting the quality of British justice and the integrity of British policemen – and that was exactly the sort of language the IRA talked. Writing about the Birmingham Six in a way that suggested they just might be innocent was seen as tantamount to giving aid and comfort to the people who had killed 21 people in two Birmingham pub bombings on that awful night in November 1974. And if any journalist had any doubt about the professional consequences of travelling down that path, there was always Conor Cruise O'Brien, the architect of the 1976 version of Section 31, around to remind them. On one famous occasion he had described *Hibernia*, one of the very few organs that did cover stories like the Birmingham Six, as a cross between the *Good Wine Guide* and *An Phoblacht*, the IRA's weekly paper.

By contrast, so-called responsible journalists, who not by coincidence were also the most successful journalists, paraded their support for censorship as a testament to their loathing of everything associated with the IRA and as an indicator of the trust that their employers (and the Government) could place in them.

When I joined *Hibernia* I discovered that some journalists would brag about how they refused to cover stories directly associated with the Provisionals. The then political correspondent of *The Irish Times*, Dick Walsh, told colleagues he would never report on the Ard Fheis or annual conference of Provisional Sinn Féin, the political arm of the IRA, on the grounds that to do so would be to treat them as a 'normal' political party. He wasn't the only mainstream reporter to ignore Sinn Féin. Walsh was right. Sinn Féin was not a normal party; it was the political arm of the IRA, whose violence had turned Ireland upside down. This, alone, surely demanded that it be exposed to media scrutiny, and perhaps more scrutiny than other parties, rather than be ignored or boycotted. Not least, there was a distinct possibility that civil society in Ireland, or at least that influential part of it that read *The Irish Times*, might benefit from an insight into what made such people tick.

I soon discovered that, on an individual level, this sort of behaviour was routine among my reporting colleagues, some of whom cast their nets widely – not only did many of them refuse to have anything to do with any Provos, but they ignored other sources who would be regarded as coming from the same ideological area, even if they were not members of the IRA or Sinn Féin. In such ways was the journalistic commitment to fostering understanding eroded and, via self-censorship and fear, Section 31's influence extended from the broadcast media to all media in Ireland.

Not all journalists took this lying down. There were editors and reporters who resisted censorship in both its forms and fought back. Some day a monument should be erected in their honour, for the truth is that in their lifetimes they suffered terribly – professionally, financially and personally – while elsewhere mediocrity thrived. The other truth is that many more were terrified of standing up to the censors, and a few actually grew to like censorship or to develop a loyalty to it, in a sort of Section 31 version of the Stockholm Syndrome.

ii

The best example of the latter occurred in 1988. After it had been on the statute books unchallenged for 17 years, Section 31 was referred to the European Commission of Human Rights in Strasbourg by the National Union of Journalists. This was an initiative taken not in Dublin but by the British branch of the union which, for historical reasons, organised in both countries, and had been spurred to action by a similar measure introduced by Margaret Thatcher's Government. In all the years of its existence prior to this, no-one in the Irish section had ever thought it necessary to challenge Section 31 in Europe.

Taking a case to the Commission requires an individual citizen of the relevant state to submit a complaint that his or her human rights have been breached by a particular law. But the NUJ soon discovered that this was something easier said than done. Not one single mainstream journalist in Dublin could be persuaded to put their name to the complaint, and the union was forced to travel to Galway on the far west coast of Ireland to find a candidate, Eoghan Ó Tuairisc, who worked for the local office of the Irish language radio station Radió na Gaeltachta.[1]

Twenty-four hours after the NUJ announced that it was taking Section 31 to Strasbourg, the chairman of the NUJ branch in the state broadcaster RTÉ, which was most adversely affected by the law, resigned in protest at what he described as this 'knee-jerk' decision by the union leadership. Charlie Bird, now the station's chief news correspondent, went on to resign from the union itself, while the RTÉ branch issued a press statement deploring 'the failure of the National Executive Committee to consult the union's membership in RTÉ before deciding to initiate a legal action which had fundamental implications for all its members'.[2]

Charlie Bird later gave newspaper interviews in which he declared his opposition to Section 31, but puzzled union colleagues in Britain and Ireland were left wondering why someone would say they opposed censorship, but then object so strenuously and publicly when colleagues decided to challenge it.

Censorship in the British media was always more subtle. From very early on the powers that be relied on public criticism or private pressure on journalists and media organisations to rein in coverage. Both the BBC and, later, the Independent Broadcasting Authority instituted bureaucratic and centralised control mechanisms to ensure that programmes fell within acceptable parameters. In the BBC, for instance, programme proposals were routinely vetted by the regional bosses in Belfast or referred up to the Director-General for approval. One consequence was that a huge number of programmes, especially those that criticised British policy or sought to explain Republican motivation, failed to make it to the screen.[3]

While self-censorship was the British way, its effect was no less telling than Section 31 in one important sense. Although there was no official ban on broadcasting the views of, or carrying interviews with, either the IRA or Sinn Féin, very few ever appeared, especially after the very early years of the Troubles. Outrage had greeted such events when they did happen and broadcasters soon learned to set limits to their reporting. The result was that the British public was largely denied explanations or explorations of the motives and ideas of people fighting a war against their government.

Overt instances of direct ministerial interference were rare, although former Northern Ireland Secretary Roy Mason once famously attempted to bully the BBC into a total blackout on reporting 'terrorist activities'.[4] Informal pressure worked better and, when the broadcast media occasionally pushed the envelope to the limit, Fleet Street's right-wing tabloids could always be relied on to savage them and pull them back into line.

Direct British Government interference in the media really began when Margaret Thatcher became prime minister. A celebrated clash with the BBC over a cancelled *Panorama* programme about the IRA was followed by a major confrontation in 1985, when pressure from the then Home Secretary, Leon Brittain, forced the BBC to cancel an interview with Martin McGuinness, an action that prompted a 24-hour strike by BBC journalists.

While censorship was not as deeply embedded in Britain as it was in Ireland, and was more often resisted, it had nonetheless become an accepted part of media coverage of the Troubles. So it was that, when Margaret Thatcher imposed the broadcasting ban of 1988, which suppressed the voices of Irish paramilitary and their political representatives on the airwaves altogether, it hardly came as a bolt out of the blue. An initial period of media resistance and indignation was followed by efforts to subvert or bypass the ban – principally by using actors to provide voice-overs for interviews with paramilitary groups – but then journalists settled down to living more-or-less happily with official censorship. The broadcasting ban became part of the media furniture.

Margaret Thatcher's ban has to be judged a success for her government. Neither journalists nor media organisations were able, or wanted badly enough, to remove it, and it stayed on the statute book until the peace process made it obsolete, along with Section 31. Meanwhile the ban succeeded in one of its main aims: coverage of the IRA and Sinn Féin, the ban's principal targets, dropped off dramatically. Sinn Féin's publicity department reported a fivefold drop in media requests in the months after the ban was introduced, a decline that became the norm, while far from resisting the ban, many journalists just gave up reporting on the Provos.[5]

So in both Britain and Ireland the tradition of aggressive, independent investigative journalism about politics and violence in Northern Ireland was largely moribund when the peace process began. The most important and far-reaching political change in Anglo–Irish relations thus got under way just as large chunks of the media in both countries had become accustomed to not asking the hard questions when it came to events in Northern Ireland, and in fact regarded the practice as risky, career-damaging and ultimately pointless.

Supporters of censorship in Ireland, such as Conor Cruise O'Brien, have argued that if either the Irish or British states had allowed the IRA and Sinn Féin unfettered access to the airwaves during the Troubles, this would have bestowed a legitimacy on the use of conspiratorial violence that no democratically elected government could allow without inviting its own destruction.[6] In other words, permitting Sean MacStiofain or Gerry Adams to appear on RTÉ to talk about the IRA's violence would have risked excusing the IRA and boosting support for it.

That is the argument of the politician, or even the policeman. It is not, or rather it should not be, the view of the reporter or editor. The media exist to tell society what is going on, to challenge power structures of all types when necessary, and to hold accountable those in the public eye and whose activities affect society, whether Conor Cruise O'Brien or Gerry Adams.

Those who work in the media should always aim to tell as much of the story as they can discover without fear or favour. To accept voluntarily limits or restrictions on this duty would be rather like a doctor deciding not to treat certain diseases, or a lawyer refusing a client because of the colour of his skin. It just should not happen. In times of conflict and communal division, such as those visited upon Northern Ireland for much of the latter half of the twentieth century, it is even more important that the media should hold firm to these values.

This is the purist journalistic stance on censorship. It is perhaps a Utopian view, but a good yardstick nonetheless. But there is another more civic-based reason why in general, and in the particular case of the Northern Ireland Troubles, censorship should be resisted. In the long term it doesn't work. It can actually be counter-productive.

iii

Allowing censorship had a number of consequences that I firmly believe made the Troubles worse and caused them to last longer than they should have. At the very least, barring the IRA and Sinn Féin from the airwaves reinforced their own sense of isolation from the rest of Irish society. They were therefore denied exposure to the forces and arguments that could have challenged them. Not only that, the Provos could justifiably accuse Britain and Ireland of hypocrisy, as their own forces were as guilty of immoral violence as they were but were never punished in the same way. In the minds of Sinn Féin and the IRA in those days, censorship strengthened the view that violence was a legitimate and perhaps the only possible response.

The media themselves were often the worst offenders in this regard. In the late 1980s a number of local correspondents from print and broadcast media organisations from both parts of Ireland briefly ran a lunch club in Belfast, to which notable players in the Troubles would be invited. The idea was that, after a good feed, the politician, policeman or whoever would take part in an off-the-record question-and-answer session designed to allow everyone to speak freely and candidly.

At the end of one lunch, the topic of conversation turned to future guests. Someone suggested inviting Gerry Adams. When the laughter died down, the argument against that won the day was the absence of a suitable restaurant in west Belfast in which to host the event. In truth, that was just an excuse. Many of the reporters in the room had never spoken to Adams and would be horrified at the thought. They were also terrified of the wider reaction if it became known that they had actually broken bread with him. It was a little like American journalists being offered, but refusing, the opportunity to quiz Osama bin Laden for a couple of hours for fear of what Fox News and the White House would say if they found out.

It was a missed opportunity for sure. Adams was in the midst, as we know now, of helping put together the peace process. But Belfast's finest let it go. Attitudes like this meant that, when the story broke years later, it came as a total surprise to many in the Irish media and to the Irish public they were supposed to keep well informed.

Among the various examples of this warping self-censorship that leap to mind, one episode stands out. That was Sinn Féin's success in the 1982 Assembly elections, the first time the party stood on its own platform rather than through surrogates such as hunger strikers. Sinn Féin won around 10% of the vote, or over 40% of the Nationalist vote. The result, which launched the Armalite and Ballot Box strategy, literally stunned Irish society, to most of whom this performance came as a bolt out of the blue.

At the time I was Northern Editor of *The Irish Times* and our office, I am still proud to say, was the only part of the Irish media that got the story right. Every other newspaper and media outlet took more-or-less the same line, one that was rooted less in reality than in wishful thinking: there was no way that Sinn Féin would do well because no-one in their right mind would vote for people who supported, organised and excused the IRA's violence. Anything else opened up too appalling and unacceptable a vista.

Our office had got the story right, but that wasn't difficult to do. Northern Ireland had just gone through the hunger strikes: the emotional bruises to the Nationalist political psyche were still visible and raw. Not only that, but anyone who spent any time covering the Provos would have to be blind, deaf and stupid not to realise that the IRA had survived as long as it had because it had roots and support in the communities whence it sprang. It was obvious that Sinn Féin would do well – the only unanswered question in our office was, how well?

I can only guess at why the rest of the media got the story so wrong. Did they know so little about the Provos? Or not want to write or say things that would be controversial and unpopular with their editors? These are questions only they can answer – although the genuine shock and surprise I encountered among many colleagues after the result suggests it was probably the former.

About 4 years afterwards, a senior colleague in *The Irish Times* told me of the turmoil our coverage of the story had caused within the paper's management. A few days before the poll I had been interviewed on RTÉ radio along with the Social Democratic and Labour Party leader John Hume, and when asked I suggested that Sinn Féin would definitely win three seats to the Assembly, probably five and possibly seven. Hume sharply disagreed. In the event they won five seats. So appalled were *The Irish Times* top brass at this interview that it was made clear at that level that, if I was wrong, I would be out of the Belfast office so fast my feet wouldn't touch the ground. When I was told this story, I couldn't help but think of the reporters who had really got the story wrong but who had faced no such punishment – but then they got the story wrong for the right reasons.

These two stories illustrate another downside of the censorship experience in Northern Ireland. It denied Irish and British society the chance to be enlightened about the character, make-up, weaknesses, strengths, motivation, aspirations, ideology and ambitions of those involved in violence, in a way that significantly mitigated against insightful and astute thinking in the centres of power in London and Dublin. Instead, I believe it produced bad government policy. In short, censorship deprived the public of the knowledge and understanding needed to make sure government made good decisions.

If there had been real, living journalism in Ireland, instead of a boring stenography of violence, how much sooner might the peace process have happened? If everyone in Ireland was talking to and about each other freely, how much earlier could we have had the ceasefires?

iv

Having said that, there is little doubt that the timidity censorship had instilled in so much of Irish journalism by the early 1990s worked to the advantage of the peace process when it did get going.

A reluctance to ask hard questions or to probe much beneath the surface suited everyone, especially the Adams–McGuinness leadership and the British and Irish governments. From the outset the process was characterised as the product of talks between Gerry Adams and the SDLP leader John Hume that had started in the late 1980s, faltered, and then resumed in the early 1990s. The two men produced a paper, the so-called 'Hume–Adams document', the contents of which were kept a tightly guarded secret, but which was said to contain the formula for peace if only the British Government would implement it.

The real story was much more complex. The roots of the peace process go back to the 1981 hunger strikes and to the election victories of Bobby Sands and his colleagues. The electoral strategy launched thereafter by the Sinn Féin leadership set Gerry Adams and his closest colleagues on a journey whose end point would be the abandonment of IRA violence and the embrace of constitutional politics.

This journey could not be completed without the Provos performing huge ideological u-turns, not the least of which was the acceptance of something that challenged the very *raison d'être* of the Provisional Republican idea: the principle that Northern Ireland's place in the United Kingdom would not change without the consent of its people.

It is no exaggeration to say that if, in the 1980s, Adams had gone to his colleagues on the Army Council and laid out the peace process in these terms – that the process would end with IRA leaders as Ministers in a government with Unionists while the IRA would decommission its weapons and go out of business – he would have been lucky to have survived the experience.

Moving the IRA towards the peace process, ceasefire, decommissioning and ultimately disbandment required more subtle tactics, ranging from sleight of hand to outright deception. Had the true direction or terminus of this journey become evident to rank-and-file IRA and Sinn Féin members at this time, the entire process could have been derailed and the lives of Adams and his colleagues put in danger. That never happened, and one very important reason was that the media shied away from digging too deeply into the story. Many reporters would drop a story if they thought it had the potential to undermine Adams's stewardship of the IRA and thereby endanger the process. Whether they did this out of fear of the personal consequences, or because the attainment of peace came before everything, doesn't really matter.

A few others, myself included, persevered regardless and set out to put the process under the closest scrutiny, not least because, as journalists, we had no option: an extraordinary event like the peace process demanded more than usual investigation if our readers were truly to understand what was going on. We may have thought we were just doing our job, but the old habits of the Irish media die hard.

Some of our colleagues – and not a few in government – branded us as 'unhelpful'; one hostile *Irish Times* reporter even coined a name for us, Journalists Against the Peace Process (JAPPs). It was a bizarre, if inverted, rerun of the criticism of the 1970s and 1980s. Back then reporters like myself were reviled for legitimising the IRA and Sinn Féin by writing about them too often; now we were undermining them by doing the same. It was clear that a good journalist, a 'helpful' reporter, should limit his or her activity to merely recording the events of the day.

As I write this the peace process, its beginning dated by the first ceasefire of 1994, has lasted nearly three times longer than the First World War, almost twice as long as the Second World War, and virtually as long as American involvement in Vietnam. Not only is the peace process in Northern Ireland one of the longest in human history, but the political stability it promised is as far off as ever, and in its stead extremism has triumphed.

Moderate Unionist trust in the process has evaporated, and Protestants have flocked to support a party whose founder and everlasting leader combines the worst elements of religious and political extremism – one who built his career on bigotry, division, fear and conflict and many of whose apparatchiks behave like mindless, loyal bullies.

The majority of Nationalists now support a party that is morally bankrupt, whose leaders lie outrageously and who stand accused of the most heinous deeds, from disappearing a widowed mother to contriving the deaths of hunger-striking comrades to advance their own political ambitions. Each has grown fat on the back of community division spawned by a peace process that seems never to end, spurred on by two governments whose leaders behave as if they care less for the sort of society they are helping to create, and much more about their own place in the history books.

Fundamental to the political prosperity of Sinn Féin and the DUP has been the failure of the peace process to produce political stability. The pattern has been repeated endlessly, to the benefit of both.

Not knowing or understanding what Adams's real agenda was, and believing it prudent to fear the worst, Unionists demanded proof of Sinn Féin's *bona fides* in the form of IRA decommissioning. Claiming that Adams was not yet secure enough to disarm his military wing, the Provos responded by stalling and cavilling over IRA weapons while allowing the IRA to rob banks and smuggle guns in such a brazen way it could only add to Unionist distrust.

Unionists argued that all this showed that the Provos just couldn't be trusted, while Sinn Féin countered that the Unionists' inherent bigotry would never allow them to share power with them. A spiral of doubt and distrust was thus created and even connived at. The two communities sought comfort and strength by flocking to their most inflexible representatives, and Sinn Féin and the DUP grew in electoral strength. Both parties had a vested interest in the process not succeeding.

The media played a crucial role in all this. By the time the Good Friday Agreement was negotiated in 1998, there was absolutely no doubt about a number of things. First, it was clear that those Unionists who suspected the peace process to be just a clever trick to achieve Irish unity were badly mistaken. It was obvious that Gerry Adams was leading the IRA and Sinn Féin into perhaps the most ambitious and far-reaching compromise in Republican history. Not only that, but the end game was clearly visible: the disbandment of the IRA, the decommissioning of its weapons, the absorption of Sinn Féin fully into constitutional politics, and the acceptance by their leaders of a state they had set out to destroy some 30 years earlier would be only a matter of time and management.

The only outstanding question, whether Adams and McGuinness were the masters of Republicanism in Northern Ireland, was settled that summer when, in a joint operation, the Real and Continuity IRA along with the Irish National Liberation Army blew 29 innocent civilians in Omagh to eternity, along with their own credibility as dissident rivals.

In the course of all my journalistic work on the peace process, in particular while researching my book on the IRA, I never once met a Republican activist who had any real doubt after 1998 about where Adams was leading the Provos. A smattering were angry about it, some welcomed it, and others were resigned to it. But after Omagh there were very few who could see any point in taking up arms against it. The Adams–McGuinness leadership was secure and no revelation from the media, no matter how sensational, about the origins of the peace process would change that.

v

In the crucial months and years after the Good Friday Agreement, when the power-sharing government was being constructed, but as often falling apart over the decommissioning issue, the media should have told this story but too often didn't, preferring instead to portray Adams's leadership as vulnerable to dissidents and unable to move as far and as fast as the Unionist leadership demanded. They were stuck in the censorship rut; unwilling to tell the story most of them knew to be true for fear of being criticised as 'unhelpful' or 'pro-dissident', of wanting to see the Adams leadership consumed by enemies.

The handling of two stories tells the tale. One was decommissioning, the issue the Adams leadership used to lever David Trimble out of power and Sinn Féin into electoral dominance of Northern Nationalism. For many of the post-Good Friday Agreement years, much of the media accepted without question the Provo assertion that decommissioning would never and could never happen, even though the logic of the peace process, and the absurdity of Sinn Féin being in government while running a well equipped private army on the side, made it both inevitable and necessary.

The media need only have probed a little into the IRA's internal affairs to discover that, whatever Sinn Féin's spin doctors told reporters, many IRA members had compelling reasons to believe that their leaders were actively planning for decommissioning to happen. But most of them didn't do this, not least because it would have entailed talking to those opposed to Adams's strategy – and that would once again have earned them the dreaded 'unhelpful' or 'pro-dissident' labels. The fact that, instead, the media gave Sinn Féin's claims such unquestioning credence contributed significantly to Unionist distrust of the Provos, and arguably that is exactly what Sinn Féin intended.

The other story was the IRA's continuing involvement in illegal activity – from robberies and gun-running to swapping arms technology for cocaine cash in Colombia – in the years after the Good Friday Agreement of 1998, a feature of life in Northern Ireland that added enormously to Unionist distrust of the process.

Too often, most of the media were happy to follow the British and Irish governments on this issue. Both London and Dublin had decided to turn a blind eye to IRA operations on the grounds that this activity kept Adams's 'hard men' in the IRA happily busy and that, with the passage of time, they would be sidelined.

Implicit in this was the view that Adams's control of the IRA was weaker than it appeared, a dubious contention to say the least. But the truth of that doesn't matter. A paramilitary group on ceasefire and committed to peaceful ways shouldn't be robbing warehouses, and the media should have been exposing this to the world every time it happened. That most of them didn't both destabilised Unionism and persuaded the Sinn Féin leadership they could get away with almost anything. If the take from the Northern Bank had been more modest, they probably would have.

It is impossible to say whether more honest journalism would have made a difference, but it might have. Is it possible that a better informed Unionist electorate, one made aware by the media of the huge compromises that Adams was making, might have been more ready to temper demands for IRA decommissioning, and more willing to believe that the war had ended on terms they previously could only have dreamed about? Would it have made any difference if the Provos had been put under greater scrutiny and their more flagrant lying exposed? And if all that had happened, would the power-sharing executive at Stormont have survived, and with it the centre ground of Northern Ireland politics?

There is no definitive answer to those questions. But there is no doubt that the political future of Northern Ireland is a pretty bleak one, notwithstanding the fact that the worst violence is over. If the power-sharing executive at Stormont is ever re-established, its leadership will probably be drawn from Sinn Féin and the DUP, the two most undemocratic, authoritarian, ruthless parties in Northern Ireland, both characterised by an unhealthy leadership cult. Nor is there any doubt that an unwillingness on the part of the media to tell the story as it was, even if that meant publishing stories that 'damaged the peace process', played no small part in bringing this dismal prospect about.

Endnotes

[1] Horgan, John (2002) Journalists and censorship: a case history of the NUJ in Ireland and the broadcasting ban 1971–74. *Journalism Studies* 3: 377–392.

[2] *Ibid.*

[3] Curtis, Liz (1984) *Ireland – The Propaganda War*. London: Pluto Press, pp. 279–290.

[4] *Ibid*, p. 138.

[5] Moloney, Ed (1991) Closing down the airwaves. In: Rolston, Bill (ed.) *The Media and Northern Ireland*. London: Macmillan, pp. 47–48.

[6] O'Brien, Conor Cruise (2005) Broadcasting and violence; the case for media restriction. In: Corcoran, Mary P. and O'Brien, Mark (eds) *Political Censorship and the Democratic State: The Irish Broadcasting Ban*. Dublin: Four Courts Press, pp. 31–32.

Ivana Bacik

Ivana Bacik is Reid Professor of Criminal Law at Trinity College Dublin, and also a practising barrister. She taught previously at the University of Kent, the University of North London and the National College of Ireland. She has written extensively on criminal law, criminology, equality and human rights law, and was Editor of the Irish Criminal Law Journal *from 1997 to 2003. She co-authored the first major report on gender discrimination in the legal professions in Ireland (Bacik I., Drew, E. and Costello, C., 2003,* Gender InJustice: Feminising the Legal Professions?*) and is author of* Kicking and Screaming: Dragging Ireland into the Twenty-First Century. *She was a candidate for the Labour Party in the 2004 European elections in Dublin; is a regular media contributor; and has been involved in numerous civil liberties, human rights and feminist campaigns.*

The Hybrid Generation
Ivana Bacik

A Personal Introduction

Identity is a strange thing. All of us have multiple identities, often contradictory, always difficult to pigeonhole. Take my generation of Irish people, the thirtysomethings, born in the late 1960s or early 1970s. We have a particularly complex identity, and have been subjected to numerous different labels or attempts at pigeonholing. Sometimes we are called the 'successor generation'; we have been described as the 'Pope's children'; we are the first social group in Ireland to experience the bizarre phenomenon of 'middle youth' or 'kidulthood'; that time in the late 20s and early 30s when our parents were married with children, but we party on like teenagers.

We are under 40 – we came of age in the late 1980s – too old to be cubs of the Celtic Tiger, old enough to remember recession and to have experienced the lean times. So we remember the days when Irish unemployment figures were close to 20%. Many of us emigrated then to find work, to Britain or the USA – but many were able to return home later, to become the key beneficiaries of the new Irish prosperity. So we have a difficult and disjointed sense of self. And our attitudes towards and relationship with our neighbouring island are as complex and contradictory as our own sense of identity.

Like so many of this hybrid Irish generation, I have strong personal connections with Britain. I was born in south London in 1968. My parents were living there at the time, having left Ireland for my father's work. We returned to Ireland when I was 6 years old. Those early, barely remembered years spent in London were romanticised when we were children living in Cork in the retelling of my mother's stories: about the excitement of being in such a big city, meeting neighbours and friends from many different ethnicities and countries, that sheer sense of life evident in the capital of the swinging sixties.

Later, however, growing up in grim 1980s Dublin, most people my age developed much more ambivalent feelings about Britain. For the young, educated, middle-class Irish of that pre-Ryanair time, British cities in general, and London in particular, were seen as places of opportunity and escape, of jobs and money – yet we were aware that they had also become places of drudgery, hostility and hopelessness for many of our fellow citizens.

As students in the 1980s, we spent our summer holidays working in London in bars and restaurants, living in overcrowded bedsits with other Irish, many of whom worked in construction and only socialised in 'County Kilburn'. Like those disadvantaged Irish labourers, we students were the butt of anti-Irish jokes, living in what often felt like a hostile place. Male friends were routinely strip-searched under the Prevention of Terrorism Act when coming across on the ferry through Holyhead. Margaret Thatcher was still in power, the Birmingham Six and Guildford Four cases were ongoing.

Yet England was still a place of hope and opportunity, not just for students looking for a way to earn their fees and living expenses for the academic year ahead – but for many other escapees from Ireland: young gay people from rural communities; women with crisis pregnancies seeking abortions or planning to stay abroad long enough to have the baby and give it up for adoption; all those desperate to get away from the stifling small towns and repressive Catholic culture with which they had grown up in pre-prosperity Ireland.

The first summer I spent working in London was 1986. A friend and I headed off, aged just 18, after finishing our first year of college, to go and work as waitresses in a pizza restaurant in Soho. We rented a bedsit in Cricklewood with a houseful of other young Irish – a mix of builders' labourers and students, presided over by an obnoxious landlord from west of the Shannon who extracted vast amounts of rent from his fellow citizens in return for pitiful living conditions in a warren of tiny houses spread throughout north London. Even this bleak reality could not detract from the wild excitement of finally living away from home, earning money and going out clubbing in glamorous places in Soho and the West End.

That summer, and the others that followed, shaped our often rose-tinted views of London as students. As left-wing student activists at Trinity College, we lamented the absence of a real ideological divide in Irish party politics at the time. We longed for the presence of a strong socialist political organisation in Ireland, and took our inspiration from the leading lights of the Labour Party in Britain. One of the proudest moments of my student life was meeting the greatest of these – Tony Benn MP – when he came to speak at a meeting we organised at Trinity. A formidable intellect, he delivered a rousing speech and wished us luck with the various campaigns we were involved in: an exhilarating moment.

Meanwhile, anyone we knew who had already graduated had either left Ireland to find work abroad, or was on the dole in Dublin. So the natural thing on finishing college was to move to London. I spent some years living there after graduation – wonderful, liberating, enlightening years, doing postgraduate studies at the London School of Economics; training to be a barrister; working in a range of different jobs; going on political protests against Margaret Thatcher, against the poll tax, against racism; partying in clubs, squats and warehouses; meeting a wide range of new people. I thought of myself as a Londoner – enjoying life immensely, rarely leaving the city to visit any other part of Britain, but still experiencing strange pangs of homesickness every time I returned to Dublin to see family and friends.

Cultural Shifts

During the time I lived in London, a perceptible shift occurred. Attitudes towards one another among both Irish and British people began to change. Ireland became a more confident society, just as a certain tiredness and loss of energy seemed to steal over London. Visits home to Dublin indicated that a new economic affluence was beginning to penetrate, and at the same time social attitudes were changing visibly. The election of Mary Robinson as President in 1990 was followed by the outraged public reaction to the X case in 1992, when thousands of people marched on O'Connell street in Dublin to protest against a High Court decision prohibiting a 14-year-old rape victim from travelling to England to obtain an abortion.

With the election of a new Fianna Fáil/Labour government in Ireland in November of that year, following swiftly on the hugely disappointing defeat of Neil Kinnock's Labour Party in the British general election some months before, the writing was on the wall for any Irish leftie still living in London.

Time to move home again, away from John Major's recession-hit Britain, back to a country that was clearly on the way up – and apparently going left.

Despite these changes and being glad to be home, I missed London immensely for years after I came back. Every time I go there now for work, to see friends or just for fun, I feel again that intense excitement, the powerful adrenalin rush of being anonymous in a big city surrounded by huge potential and energy. Under New Labour, London has really blossomed again. The developments lining the south of the Thames in London: the Tate Modern, the London Eye and Ken Livingstone's fabulous City Hall are key signs of exciting physical change. Since 1997 British society has been greatly reinvigorated: a greater economic and cultural confidence has returned with the Blair government, the birth of so-called 'Cool Britannia', and the redevelopment of so many urban centres. But although many changes have occurred in Britain in recent years, undoubtedly Ireland has changed more, and more fundamentally. In particular, we have stopped being the 'poor relations', both within Europe and in our dealings with Britain. This tremendous shift in the power dynamic between Ireland and Britain began to happen, I believe, in the years when the British economy slumped in the dying days of the last Tory regime, and when the Irish economy simultaneously began to reassert itself, as paramilitary ceasefires held and peace became a reality in Northern Ireland.

This process was already in train when I returned home in the mid-1990s, matched by the shift in attitudes that was becoming evident even then. Since that time, we have become more and more confident in Ireland as the boom has continued and the peace process winds on. This immense social and attitudinal transformation has manifested itself in many ways, some tangible, some less so. Most of the changes have been very positive, although unfortunately our new-found prosperity has also had some negative side effects.

Changes in Irish Society

Tangible and hugely positive signs of change in Ireland are apparent in the vastly increased rates of women's participation in the labour force; the increasingly diverse forms of family life; the enhanced visibility of the gay community; and the growth of new communities drawn from other countries.

A major factor driving the economic boom over recent years has been the rise in female labour force participation – the proportion of women in employment has risen dramatically over the past decade. Between 1995 and 2000, the single biggest factor contributing to the rise in labour supply was increased female participation, estimated as contributing 1.5% a year to the growth in potential output of the economy.

The 1990s generally must be acknowledged as having marked a very positive stage in the development of feminism in Ireland: a great move forward in the liberation of women economically, socially and sexually, with mainstreaming of the concept of gender equality through legislative and policy developments. Irish women have made very considerable advances in that relatively short time. We have had two women presidents since 1990; a woman is currently Tánaiste in the Government; two of eight Supreme Court judges are now women; and ordinary women are more independent, more liberated and more in control of their own lives than ever before in our history.

A similar sea-change has occurred with the increased acceptance of lesbian and gay people in Irish society. Until 1993 it was a criminal offence to engage in consensual homosexual intercourse. Since decriminalisation and the passing of enlightened anti-discrimination legislation, a new generation of high-profile young gay men have become media celebrities in Ireland: Graham Norton, Brendan Courtney, Brian Dowling. A thriving gay scene is based around a number of venues and events in different urban centres, and increased political confidence has led to a common perception that homosexuality is now positively valued in Irish society. Like the feminist movement, this is a campaign that has come a long way in a short time – in just over a decade, from a criminal offence to a matter of pride.

Just as Irish attitudes towards sexuality have become more tolerant and pluralist, so a fundamental change has occurred in our family and social structures, with the numbers of those cohabiting having increased dramatically. In the 1996 Census, cohabiting couples made up only 4% of all family units; by the 2002 Census this figure had more than doubled. Couples without children constitute the type of family unit showing the fastest growth rate, up by 79% since 1981. Divorce and remarriage rates are also increasing. Since the legalisation of divorce in 1995, the number of divorced persons has more than trebled in 6 years. The percentage of births outside marriage now stands at just over 31%, almost a third of births compared with just over a quarter (25.3%) in 1996.

The shape of the family in Irish society has gone through a remarkable transformation in the last decade, but there should be no misplaced nostalgia around the demise of the traditional model. Rather, the more liberated forms of family life now emerging should be celebrated, and the myth that change is negative should be challenged. Change in family forms can and should be viewed as positive because it has come about alongside a discernible shift in social attitudes in Ireland in the past decade, marked by a greater tolerance of diversity generally. This shift has occurred for both internal and external reasons – the internal being largely economic or related to land-ownership patterns; the external being changing trends internationally. The truly interesting feature of this shift in Ireland is how new it is – only a decade old, although its origins are earlier; any divergence from the accepted model of family was still frowned upon until the late 1980s.

Now we are witnessing greater demand for, and tolerance of, personal choice regarding life and lifestyle decisions. Individuals no longer feel coerced into a prescribed social destiny, and this is a change that must be welcomed as a step forward for Irish society. Official Ireland still recognises only the traditional heterosexual family based on marriage. Yet the typical Irish family is changing rapidly as rates of cohabitation increase dramatically and society modernises. There are almost twice as many women at work today than 10 years ago; contraception has become more widely available; increasing numbers of people are cohabiting, separating, divorcing, forming new relationships, and coming out of the closet. Gay and straight people are lobbying for legal recognition for partnerships without the need for marriage; young and older people alike are rejecting traditional, unduly rigid and repressive models of family life.

With these very visible positive changes in Irish life, I believe that our cultural values and sense of identity have also changed rapidly, and largely for the better. The economic boom has made us a more confident and outward-looking society. Our social and cultural values have become more pluralist. We have become a more tolerant and diverse people, enriched by immigration and by greater diversity in every way: socially, culturally and economically. Yet many people are inclined to take a 'doomsday' view of modern Ireland. The decline in religious attendance, the apparent loss of trust in institutions such as the Catholic Church and the Government, youth drinking, apparent growth in violent crime figures, even corruption in the planning process – all these are pointed to as signs of social fragmentation. Some have even argued that with the loss of old certainties has come a 'gaping void', a loss of all values.

I disagree strongly with this view, which I believe stems from a misplaced sense of nostalgia. I think it is wrong to hark back to times past in a misguided attempt to rediscover a richer set of values. Twenty years ago, Ireland was an infinitely more miserable place than it is today: insular, narrow-minded, with little tolerance of any diversity. We had high unemployment and high emigration. We conveniently forget that even our crime figures were higher then. At the time, we simply exported our biggest social problems abroad, mostly to England – our unemployed, our dispossessed, those who did not fit into a narrowly defined social mould. For those who stayed behind, depression, suicide, child sexual abuse and alcoholism were problems just as they are now, and many older people thought the social fabric was breaking down, just as they do now. The fact is that we were not better people then – just poorer and perhaps more hypocritical.

In truth, I believe that we are better people now, that we have become a much more public-spirited, more tolerant and more community-minded society than we ever were before the boom. This belief is confirmed by recent magnificent public endeavours such as the Special Olympics, and the mass demonstrations on the streets of our cities in protest against the war in Iraq. In two important aspects, however, I think the Irish value system has not improved in recent years.

First, the economic values that have generated such wealth for a number of individuals have deeply polarised this tiger society, allowing the gap between rich and poor to widen as the price of living creeps ever higher. The reckless application of right-wing economic policies has left us with unjustifiable levels of poverty, a creaking health system and grossly underfunded public services. By any standards we have first-world per capita average income levels, but a third-world social infrastructure. Patients die on trolleys; babies are born in ambulances; children with disabilities cannot get an adequate education; homeless numbers continue to rise; nurses, teachers and public servants cannot afford homes of their own in our capital city.

Second, although one of the most positive recent changes in Irish society has been the increasing diversity of our communities, there is unfortunately a notable lack of generosity, and even a discernible racism, in the attitudes of many Irish towards the new communities springing up around the country. We have seen the return home of more and more Irish emigrants and have even become a land of net inward migration. Now we attract migrants from around the world: the professional workers from abroad; the nurses and doctors so urgently needed to staff our underfunded healthcare system; the students flocking to learn English and earn money from tips in bars and restaurants, as we used to do in London. We attract people from the poorest and most repressive countries in the world seeking political asylum and refugee status – and of course we attract dispossessed, unskilled workers from poorer countries, who come here to do jobs in construction and in the service industry that Irish people will no longer consider.

Unfortunately, we do not appear to have learned much from our own treatment in so many other countries when we were the economic migrants. This is the second negative aspect of the newly changed Ireland, and one that has become insidious and difficult to counter. Given Ireland's long history of emigration, and with the experience of living and working abroad a continued reality for many Irish people, it might be expected that once levels of immigration into this country began to rise, a welcome would be extended to those arriving here, fleeing either political persecution or economic deprivation. Unfortunately, that has not proved to be the case. Despite our traditional reputation as a friendly kind of place, the reality is that visitors here often perceive Ireland as a very unwelcoming country.

In recent years there has been a deeply worrying increase in the spread of anti-immigrant myths, racist incidents, and sometimes even violent attacks. There is little leadership from the Government on the issue, with foot-dragging over the introduction of any proper immigration policy compounding the issue, and widespread justifications of restrictive immigration policies. This lack of emphasis on the positive nature of immigration is both narrow-minded and short-sighted. We should be positively welcoming of inward migration if we are serious about wanting our Irish identity, our 'Irishness', to have an inclusive, dynamic and progressive meaning in the future.

Changing Relations with Britain

It can be argued that, given the immense social and economic changes that have occurred in this country, the meaning of being Irish has changed fundamentally over the past two decades. This is not true just for my hybrid generation of Celtic pre-tiger cubs, the thirtysomethings – it is true for Irish citizens generally, and for all those who claim to be Irish worldwide, the so-called diaspora. Our shift in identity has also had a marked effect on our relations with other countries; with the USA, within the European Union, and most especially with our nearest neighbour, Britain.

This change in Irish identity, which I personally have experienced in the past two decades, is clearly reflected in *Through Irish Eyes*, a report published by the British Council in Ireland in 2004, based on research into attitudes towards Britain among the 'successor generation' of Irish people under 40. The research confirms that my generation has a contradictory and complex attitude to Britain: we are very familiar with Britain and broadly favourable towards it as a country, but our own growing national self-confidence means that we feel Britain is less important to us now than it was.

Although we recognise how intertwined we are culturally with the British, the shift in power relations is strongly evident. A real sense emerges that, while Irish people and Irish culture are popular in Britain, and the British want us to like them, this does not seem to apply in the same way the other way around. Irish boy bands top the British charts, Irish writers dominate the bestseller lists, Irish comedians, presenters and reality show contestants take English audiences by storm. In short, it seems we do pop culture much better than the Brits, even if in this sphere they have taught us everything we know.

The conclusion must be that, in the past 20 years, Ireland has moved from post-colonial to cultural partner status as far as Britain is concerned. No longer the underdog, we are content to be top dog culturally and morally, basking smugly in the Eurozone and in the envy of our EU neighbours, lapping up investment from US multinationals, and having the best of both Boston and Berlin.

Our relationship with Britain, characterised perhaps by the excellent working relationship of the current Irish Taoiseach and British Prime Minister on the peace process, is now based on mutual respect between equal partners. So, might you be forgiven for thinking that we are getting close to seeing Britain as just another foreign country? Well, yes, except that, unlike any other foreign country, deep down we still really hate to see them getting knocked out of the World Cup. Where is the fun if England is not playing, so we can cheer in support of whoever is playing against them?

The Debate about Identity

More seriously, for too long Irish identity has invariably been defined in contrast to that of our nearest geographical neighbour. Despite our new-found self-confidence, in many respects the obsession over our history with Britain remains unchanged. That it is now cool to be Irish in Britain does not alter the fact that people in Britain know much less about Ireland than we know about them. We know all about British pop culture and British politics; implicit in much of our education is the concept of Britain as the norm and Ireland as the 'other'.

When teaching law in Irish universities, for example, we still refer extensively to English cases, House of Lords decisions and British legislation. The same is not true of British law students, who remain blithely unaware of important and relevant decisions in the Irish courts. Even today, Irish law textbooks routinely have the word 'Ireland' or 'Irish' in the title, to justify their existence ('Irish Land Law'; 'The Law of Contract in Ireland'). By contrast, English law books simply bear the subject title: 'Criminal Law' or 'Land Law', asserting by implication that there is only one jurisdiction, the norm by which others are measured. Of course this is changing, particularly as we are now just two out of 25 jurisdictions within an enlarged and greatly empowered EU legal system. Nonetheless, in many ways we continue to refer and defer to Britain. Now that we have become more self-confident, it is appropriate that we should move beyond this obsession and begin to define ourselves on our own terms. Yet in this country we have never had a proper debate about the meaning of 'Irishness'.

This will change. I caught a glimpse recently of the shape such a debate could take, in a context other than Irish–British relations. In 2003, along with a number of Irish academics and policymakers, I was invited to attend a conference entitled 'Re-imagining Ireland,' held in Charlottesville, Virginia, USA. This was an extraordinary event. Funded by the Virginia State Department of the Humanities, the speakers were all flown over from Ireland; but the audience, the majority of whom were over 50, was exclusively drawn from the Irish-American diaspora. During the fascinating debates between and among the invited speakers over different aspects of Irish culture and society, there emerged from the audience a distinct sense of puzzlement, a clear indication that they were not hearing what they had expected to hear: that their strong sense of Irishness, nurtured over many generations in a foreign country, was being challenged by these upstarts from the old sod. It seems that members of the Irish diaspora in the USA have never experienced a serious shift in their own sense of identity: they are strangely confident about their Irishness, yet it is rooted in an outdated vision of Ireland, a John Hinde postcard view, unrecognisable in today's Celtic Tiger.

For instance, after a lengthy debating session in which Irish commentators animatedly discussed the problems – of poverty, drug abuse, long-term unemployment – among disadvantaged urban communities in Dublin, Cork and Limerick, one of the audience members asked rather querulously: 'But what about rural poverty, what about the smallholder in rural Ireland?' Clearly, brought up as they had undoubtedly been on stories of the Famine and the desperate plight of the cottier and smallholder classes, the idea that urban poverty might be more of an issue nowadays was foreign to them.

Similar unease was expressed by those audience members present at the screening of *Goldfish Memory*, a film depicting the wild lives and complex love interests of a group of young gay and straight people in today's Dublin. One elderly Irish-American asked plaintively if there were really that many gay people in Ireland? You could sense slight embarrassment at audience reactions like these among those of us there as speakers, the urban intellectuals, there to represent the new Ireland, yet presented with such unwelcome reminders of where we had come from so recently. It reminded me of the embarrassment my Irish grandmother expressed when I asked her about whether her grandparents had ever talked about the Famine; or the embarrassment collectively felt by older relatives when the subject of the 1916 Easter Rising comes up. So much of our relatively recent history remains a source of shame to us, based on a real revulsion at what the independence movement became, repugnance for the tactics of the IRA in the 1970s and 1980s, and a genuine empathy with their victims of violence in Britain and Northern Ireland. This shame and embarrassment have hampered any real debate about the meaning of Irish identity.

By contrast (and we can't help making this contrast), a serious debate is well under way on the meaning of a national identity in Britain. In January 2006, British Chancellor Gordon Brown put forward the idea of an annual British Day to celebrate 'British history, achievements and culture'. His suggestion generated a great deal of controversy, many commentators pointing out that, given Britain's colonial past and the very different ethnicities of its present-day citizens, a large-scale celebration of this kind might only cause further division. But the debate itself is vitally important, particularly in the wake of the horrific London bombings of July 2005. In this aftermath, the debate about Britishness has assumed a new significance. As Brown said, those events may be seen as an extreme example of what can happen if groups of people feel they have little in common with, or bear no allegiance to, the larger community within which they were born and raised.

A similar debate about national identity should be taking place in Ireland in the light of the rapid and fundamental changes that have occurred in this country. Some indication that it might soon be undertaken is apparent in the reaction to a speech made by President Mary McAleese, also in January 2006, on the subject of the 1916 Rising. There was much hostile reaction to her suggestion that the Rising was not an exclusive or sectarian enterprise, to her depiction of the heroes of the Rising as 'Davids to their [the British Empire's] Goliaths', and to her recommendation that we should reclaim Irish nationalism. The hostility towards this viewpoint is, I am sure, based on the general embarrassment so many of us feel about Irish nationalism, a sense that a narrow form of that nationalism has been hijacked and claimed by the violent republican movement. Yet, to be fair, President McAleese, like Chancellor Gordon Brown, was only attempting to begin a long overdue debate. After all, the embarrassment we feel about Irish nationalism is very similar to the embarrassment felt by many people in Britain over the hijacking of the Union Jack by far-right groups such as the British National Party.

The truth is that, in both Ireland and Britain, nationalism is felt to be somehow shameful, and a sense of nationalist pride is never uncomplicated. That much, like so much else, is common ground between us. Perhaps my generation and younger generations, growing up with little or no memory of violent conflict in Northern Ireland, may be the first to reclaim a positive, proud and pluralist Irish identity, far from a narrow, nationalist sense, but based on a view of Ireland as independent and equal to other nations, including our neighbouring island. Perhaps, too, this reformulation of Irish identity will be mirrored by the development of a new sense of national identity, based on similar positive and pluralist values, by our contemporaries in Britain.

John A. Murphy

Born in Macroom, Co. Cork, John A. Murphy was educated at University
College, Cork, and from 1971–90 took up a professorship in Irish History there.
He lectured extensively on Irish history and politics at various US, UK, Canadian
and Australian universities, and was visiting professor on a number of university
campuses in the 1970s and 1980s. At home he became a well known media
commentator, and served as an independent member of Seanad Éireann from
1977–83 and 1987–92. He was awarded an honorary doctorate by the National
University of Ireland in 2001 for his contributions to scholarship and public
life. In 2005 his former colleagues and graduate students presented him with
a festschrift, History and the Public Sphere. Inheriting a simplistic faith-and-
fatherland doctrine, he has summed up his political philosophy as 'disentangling,
not destroying, the meshed threads of our history – the tribe from the nation;
language and culture from nationalism and physical force; and the Roman
Catholic Church from the state.'

Colonial chains, domestic links[1]
John A. Murphy

i

My native town is Macroom, situated in what I call 'inland' West Cork, my ancestral territory of West Muskerry and Uibh Laoghaire. This is the immemorial homeland of my family, small farmers and craftsmen for generations, proud and defiant survivalists. Some years ago a lecturer was pontificating about Irish mongrel genes when I pointed out authoritatively that I was a pure Gael, if you discounted a solitary and exotic Fitzgerald presence in the pedigree two centuries back.

Mine is the country of the poet Máire Bhuídhe Ní Laoghaire, whose stirring composition *Cath Chéim an Fhia* commemorates a famous episode in the agrarian resistance of 1822 to the rule of the local Protestant magistracy and gentry; and of the Catholic hero Art ó Laoghaire, whose 'uppity' pretensions had cost him his life at the hands of the same gentry in 1773, and who was immortalised by another woman poet, his widow Eibhlín Dubh Ní Chonaill, in the celebrated *caoineadh*[2]. Later on, in 1920, all this was the backdrop to the IRA 'flying column' – whose bloody ambush of a Macroom-based Auxiliary force at Kilmichael was a pivotal ballad-saluted event in the guerrilla war of independence.

This was the heritage I imbibed in song and story, in Irish and English, at home and school, as I grew up in the 1940s. Add to that my parents' involvement in the cultural and political revolution of the Gaelic League and Sinn Féin in the early twentieth century, and my own boyhood exposure to the electoral excitement and turbulence of early Fianna Fáil consolidating its power in the land. You could hardly think of a more intense nationalist formation.

And yet that was not the full story. Though my father was of artisan and Fenian stock, my mother was the daughter of a petit-bourgeois Redmondite. Her Irish-Ireland sentiments (shared with, if not largely influenced by, her husband-to-be) did not interest her siblings in the least. Nicholas Mansergh's arresting definition of Irish nationalism as 'the slowly maturing and finally indestructible conviction that Ireland should and would be free' was not evenly felt throughout the country, or by every class. The distinctions David Fitzpatrick draws are nearer the historical mark – that nationalism evoked in different individuals such contrasting reactions as enthusiasm, mild interest, irritation, betrayal and indifference. My mother's family was largely apolitical and, during the 1916–23 troubles, simply hoped that all this nationalist fervour would soon cease and that a lifestyle indistinguishable from their English counterparts could be resumed.

Much of our social life centred on my mother's piano and my boyhood was filled with songs of every description. Obviously, my parents were given to singing nationalist ballads, but there were also operatic arias, Broadway hits, English music-hall ditties and such dramatic Edwardian parlour pieces from my mother's girlhood as *Thora* and *Nirvana*. She had (I still have) three volumes of *The World's Favourite Songs*, sedate drawing-room effusions to be heard, no doubt, at that time in Hove or Hampstead as well as in Macroom. My parents were ardent Irish-Irelanders but saw nothing incongruous in belting out 'I'm Enery the Eighth, I am, I am'. And they were not at all put off by the censorious fulminations of Gaelic League zealots about 'the inanities of the anglicised music hall'.

Thus my earliest British–Irish influences were unwittingly shaped by parents who were steeped in Irish nationalism, who never travelled outside Ireland, and who frequently urged me (in song) to 'make the false Saxon feel/ Erin's avenging steel.' Today, when (as a change from *An Clár Bog Déil* or *Sliabh Geal gCua*) I give out *Mandalay* or *Pale Hands I Loved*, learnt at my mother's piano stool, I tell my fellow-singers in club or pub that they too must cherish their British heritage. The reaction is an ambivalent and uneasy chuckle. Perhaps I could convey my point in another way: my own cultural upbringing illustrates a larger historical truth – that the nineteenth- and early twentieth-century experience of the British dimension was as much domestic as colonial.

In the intensely nationalist Ireland of my boyhood, ballads, platform rhetoric and 'faith-and-fatherland' history lessons would all have me equate 'English' with 'foreign' and 'alien'. Yet other influences at home, in school and in society at large were equally teaching me the opposite. While still in primary school,

I devoured one Dickens novel after another from a small, blue-covered edition in protective glossy cellophane wraps lent to me by a local teacher. Later, a De La Salle brother, who had escaped the nationalist virus, infused us with his enthusiasm for the glories of English literature – plays, novels, essays and poetry – especially for that most universal of playwrights, Shakespeare, and that most quintessentially English of all poets, Alfred Lord Tennyson.

My light entertainment was a weekly English comic and I was a devoted Richmal Crompton fan, hungrily staring one Christmas at a new 'William' in a bookshop window, priced hopelessly beyond my reach at two shillings and sixpence. I was also to develop a life-long predilection for English humour and comedians; Tommy Cooper videos still brighten many a dull mood. English usage, phrases and idiom continue to fascinate, and Fowler and Brewer are frequently consulted.

It has been my good fortune, then, to be the continuing beneficiary of a rich and mutually enhancing bilingual tradition – *an dá arm aigne*[3], a double intellectual and cultural armoury. My four grandparents were native Irish speakers, my Gaelic League parents had only the *cúpla focal*[4], and although I grew up speaking Hiberno-English, it was only in my adult years that, by application and practice, I became a fluent Irish speaker, entering into my ancestral inheritance and experiencing a different and fulfilling dimension in speech and song.

It is here, with this bilingual experience, that we come to the heart of the British–Irish matter. My own case would be typical of generations of my countrymen since independence. It can be simply put. For me and the overwhelming majority, Irish is our ancestral, but English is our native, language. We don't like to reflect on these truths, erroneously referring to Irish as our 'native' language. But English is the language of much of the literature produced in Ireland, the language of Joyce, Shaw, Synge – and Seamus Heaney. And being our mother tongue, it is hardly surprising that we should take to English literature and to certain features of the English mind-set as expressed in the language.

Paradoxically, English is the language and the vehicle of modern Irish nationalism and of sometimes virulently anglophobic sentiment in prose and verse. Irish nationalism is grounded in the patriotic polemics and versifications of the Young Irelanders in the mid-nineteenth century. The Young Irelanders were greatly influenced by the tone and sentiments of contemporary English romantics. They unwittingly set a headline in hypocrisy for future Irish politicians by piously proclaiming – in English – the importance of learning and speaking Irish.

Irish nationalism is a function and a consequence of Anglicisation. It is difficult to see how popular nationalism could have developed, had Ireland stayed Irish-speaking. This is not only because Irish remained a peasant language, lacking the modern and technical means of propagating ideology, but because illiterate Irish-speaking communities in the early nineteenth century were not concerned with abstractions such as 'England' and 'nation'. Such concepts enter into Irish only with the advent of the Gaelic League and Irish-Ireland, when Irish nationalism had already been fully formed – in English.

As reflected in the popular poetry of Rafterí, Máire Bhuídhe Ní Laoghaire and Tomás Rua Ó Súilleabháin, our early nineteenth century Gaelic-speaking ancestors cherished pre-political millenarianism, prophecies and liberation myths, but for the most part they were preoccupied with survival against their local oppressors – landlords and their agents, tithe-proctors, magistrates and parsons – in short, the Protestant enemy. When they hailed heroes such as Daniel O'Connell, they interpreted him in their own archaic, sectarian and apocalyptic terms, much to the discomfiture of that modern, reformist, liberal politician. The very word 'sasanach' meant Protestant and local, rather than English and foreigner. In this general connection, the equation Catholic = Gaelic = nationalist is facile and unhistorical. But elaboration of that proposition must be another day's work...

ii

Moving away, for the moment, from my personal background and my Gaelic ancestors, let me reflect on the political realities of the British–Irish relationship in the early twentieth century, and on the shape of what might have been.

When the third Home Rule Bill was introduced in 1912, before the magnitude of its implications became evident, it seemed for a while that the long relationship would develop into an amicable political settlement. In legal and political terms, Home Rule meant limited devolution under the benignly vigilant eye of the imperial government. As a nationalist concept, however, Home Rule was, as has been well said, a 'beckoning Utopia'. From countless nationalist platforms over the decades, it was interpreted as ending the Union, undoing the conquest and generally providing the panacea for the country's problems. Thus a modest measure of self-government was somehow made to seem a nation once again.

The problem was that Home Rule meant one thing in Ireland and another in Britain. Its English advocates championed it in the fervent hope that it would end estrangement and strengthen the Union. Had there been no other post-1912 problems and 'events' (in Macmillan's sense of that word), such contradictory attitudes guaranteed that friction would have arisen sooner or later, as a Dublin parliament would have chafed against constitutional and financial restrictions. But in 1912, had all gone smoothly, Home Rule would have been welcomed by Irish public opinion. In the first decade of the twentieth century, for all the cultural-revolutionary stirrings in the undergrowth, Ireland was a complacent Edwardian country, accepting the benefits of constructive unionism and linked by innumerable ties with Great Britain. The archival footage of film-makers Sagar Mitchell and James Kenyon, covering various scenes in Cork City around 1903, was shown recently on Irish television and astounded viewers with its scenes of the citizens flying the Union Jack and warmly greeting royal representatives. Middle-class, urban Irish families pursued a lifestyle indistinguishable from that of their counterparts across the Irish Sea. Golf, music hall, the ballroom, West End-style theatre – England's 'masher' habits, in Archbishop Croke's contemptuous phrase – were enjoyed as much in anglicised urban Ireland as they were in Britain.

And the British Empire increasingly offered career opportunities to military and professional Irishmen. People like John Redmond believed that the Empire needed Ireland's contribution; that the proper resolution of the British–Irish relationship was bound up with the Empire; that Irish nationalism and imperial participation were perfectly compatible; and that Irish involvement in Empire would bridge the gap between nationalist and unionist.

The prospect of such a cosy scenario was shattered by the 1916 Rising and its aftermath. The apparently vindictive manner of the execution of its leaders, the sheer silliness of the German plot allegations, the 1917 convention debacle and, above all, the threat of conscription – these developments mobilised even middle Ireland and rallied moderate nationalist support for resurgent Sinn Féin, leading to the 1918 election victory, the setting up of Dáil Éireann and the separatist affirmation of an Irish Republic. During the independence struggle of 1920–21, nationalist sentiment was further embittered by Black-and-Tan and Auxiliary atrocities and the symbolism of the Crown became more alien and odious, and a stumbling block in negotiations down the road.

In spite of all this, and notwithstanding that formal nationalist demand had shifted from Home Rule to Republic, hostilities in 1920–21 were far from total and much of normal life continued, including British–Irish contacts at various levels. The Truce of July 1921 was popularly greeted with the relief that marks a return to normality rather than the jubilation that accompanies a triumph. Hope for a satisfactory accommodation rather than an expectation of outright victory reflected the general mood, and a clear majority of Irish nationalist voters backed the Treaty settlement (although imposed under duress) in elections in 1922 and 1923. The non-republican Arthur Griffith spoke for many in the Treaty debates when he reminded his colleagues of the realism behind Thomas Davis's – and his own – nationalist philosophy: 'peace with England, alliance with England to some extent and, under certain circumstances, confederation with England, but an Irish ambition, Irish hopes, strength, virtue and rewards for the Irish.'

These revolutionary years also witnessed the rapid constitutional evolution towards independence of the self-governing dominions in the British Empire. But Irish nationalists had little knowledge of, and still less interest in, this dramatic transformation. While the Treaty settlement seemed to place Ireland in this promising context (Canada being put forward as the constitutional model for the Irish Free State), thus providing a wider familial setting for the British–Irish relationship, there was little enthusiasm in nationalist Ireland, then or thereafter, for the Commonwealth dimension. Although Ireland did not formally break the link until 1949, there was never really a Commonwealth political party, for example, and moves to rejoin the Commonwealth today are sporadic, ineffectual and not taken seriously. Unlike other 'white dominions', Ireland regarded itself as a mother country. It had difficulty in accepting the Crown as Commonwealth head and, above all, its relative weakness and geographical proximity, as well as the pattern of history, made it vulnerable to interference from London in ways that did not apply to faraway Canada, South Africa and New Zealand.

Meanwhile, republicans blamed English malignity for the debacle of the Treaty split and the ensuing Civil War. In their view, a British-dictated constitution had been imposed on the Free State, and pressure had been put on Michael Collins to break the 1922 election pact with his former comrades and to attack the republican occupants of the Four Courts with British-supplied guns. In this interpretation, the Civil War was the cynical 'divide-and-rule' strategy of a Machiavellian power. The copper fastening of partition in 1925 only rounded off the betrayal of the revolution.

By 1923, despite the ringing affirmation in 1800 that the Union would last for ever, there was no longer a United Kingdom of Great Britain and Ireland. There were now two states in the British Isles, unequal in size, population and resources, and one of them not yet fully sovereign although practising the other's politico-legal system with variations. An entirely new political and diplomatic dimension had been introduced into the long relationship, which remained a complex one. There was much unfinished business. An imposed settlement would not heal the hurt of centuries overnight. But geographical and commercial realities could not be conjured away, and continuing close workaday contact between the two peoples co-existed with uneasy post-colonial feelings, at least on the part of the Irish. The tendency on the British side was to turn away, characteristically, from Irish affairs, which no longer divided British politics. For the Irish, continuing anglophobia provided self-righteous relief from the sober realities of self-government. The erstwhile wicked stepmother continued to be blamed for partition and other grievances. The *seanbhean bhocht*[5] had been *olagóning*[6] for so long that her children took some time to break the habit and grow up.

But by the mid-1920s the Irish Free State, although maimed by civil war and still lacking political consensus, was a going concern, with some firm idea of how to use constitutional stepping stones to achieve that sovereignty which national self respect demanded, and which alone could provide reconciliation with the former oppressor on a basis of equality. This objective underlay Éamon de Valera's single-minded constitutional programme from 1932 onwards. (Interestingly, de Valera was never an anglophobe and, even in the revolutionary period, was prepared to recognise English security concerns, greatly to the fury of Irish-Americans.)

The neutrality policy during the First World War was, among other things, the supreme expression of Irish sovereignty. That policy angered many British people for decades to come, an anger rekindled in some quarters by the Haughey Government's stance during the Falklands/Malvinas war in 1982. The *locus classicus* for the articulation of that anger is Churchill's victory speech in 1945, to which de Valera's riposte is renowned. In time, however, and with the disclosure of new evidence, perceptive British commentators realised that the formal protocols of neutrality were more than balanced by Irish governmental cooperation with the Allies, numerous individual Irish enlistments in the British forces, and the practical contributions to the war effort of legions of Irish workers in English hospitals and ammunition factories. In that connection, the central irony of Irish independence in the decades after 1922 was the failure of the economy to provide work for young citizens who were obliged in vast numbers to earn their living in the land of the old enemy. de Valera's promise that 'no longer shall our children, like our cattle, be brought up for export' turned out to be hollow and hypocritical. Influenced perhaps by a bizarre sense of poetic/historic justice, there was a tendency as well to let our former oppressor take care of our petty criminals. District judges often gave small-time delinquents the choice of a prison sentence or 'going to England'!

When Ireland severed its remaining links with the Commonwealth in 1949, British pragmatism and good sense prevailed: the citizens of the newly declared Republic were not treated as aliens, and the strong and multitudinous links between the two states continued to be given expression in a unique common travel area. This arrangement remained substantially undisturbed, even during the tense decades of the IRA terrorist campaign from 1970 onwards. Economic relations became closer through the free-trade agreement of 1965, which finally laid the ghost of the bitter 'economic' war of the 1930s. When both states joined the European Economic Community (today, the

European Union) in 1973, a progressive new context was provided for an increasingly close relationship: the opportunity for 'bilateral meetings' (especially on Northern Ireland matters) on the margins of EU summits has been a particularly welcome development. All this has made arguments for Ireland rejoining the Commonwealth even more unconvincing and irrelevant.

iii

Back to the present day, and quite the most extraordinary twist in the long relationship has been the evolution of what amounts to a joint policy on Northern Ireland. This could not have been remotely foreseen in the early decades after independence in 1922. By the early 2000s, radical changes had taken place in the attitudes of Dublin and London towards Northern Ireland. The Republic and Great Britain were on a much more equal footing than ever before (partly because of Ireland's enhanced international standing, notably through the UN and the EU, but also because of the economic success of the so-called Celtic Tiger), and this equality benefited the mutual relationship at a psychological level.

But it was the Northern Ireland conflict itself, from the early 1970s onwards, that eventually and unexpectedly resolved the stalemate. Both sovereign states realised they had an overriding common interest in defeating IRA terrorism, in coaxing paramilitaries along the pathways of peace, and in trying to achieve accommodation between the factions of a divided, recalcitrant and politically immature community. And so the deeply contentious issue of the 1940s became the common enterprise of the 1990s.

An important feature of the strengthening relationship between the two governments has been the personal friendship, even rapport, between successive taoisigh and prime ministers – certainly between Albert Reynolds and John Major (an improbable pairing), and much more so between Bertie Ahern and Tony Blair. A reconciliatory move towards healing historical antagonisms has been an increasing Irish willingness to salute the memory of Irish soldiers who died in British armies in two world wars. In this respect, the joint presence of Queen Elizabeth and President McAleese at Messines in November 1998 was powerfully symbolic. Wearing the British Legion poppy, however, remains a step too far for most citizens of the Republic.

Of course, there are still differences and disagreements at official political levels. Certainly, in EU terms, the interests of the two states are by no means identical. Also, in the earlier days of the Troubles, Dublin (still strongly identifying with Northern nationalists) brought allegations of British torture before European courts. More recently, there have been complaints from the Irish government that Britain hasn't been cooperating with investigations into the 1974 Monaghan/Dublin bombings, presumably because the required information would show British intelligence activities in an unfavourable light.

An ongoing source of Irish grievance is the nuclear reprocessing plant at Sellafield in Cumbria: the Irish worry about the adverse effects of its operations on the environment, in the Irish Sea and along the east coast, and about the consequences of a possible terrorist attack. Our repeated demands for the plant's closure have so far fallen on deaf British ears. But the grievance traffic is not all one way: complaints have been made to Dublin that failure to curb Irish driftnet fishery threatens UK salmon stock. However, these comparatively minor irritations are not a real threat to what I consider by far the most important of Ireland's bilateral relationships on the world stage.

How far do popular opinions and attitudes correspond to this satisfactory state of intergovernmental relations? First of all, we are talking about an 'imbalance of interest' where the plain people of the two islands are concerned. As a generalisation (but a sound one), Irish people's informed interest in British politics and culture is not reciprocated. Perhaps that is an inevitable historical and geographical feature of the relationship. Nevertheless, I've been surprised that so many affable and well travelled British people I've met in the course of continental coach tours have never been to Ireland. This was understandable during the Troubles. But perhaps there's a more general fear/ignorance factor still at work. One would imagine that sheer curiosity alone would prompt an Englishman to visit the neighbouring island. When Ireland was experiencing a false economic dawn in the 1960s, and hotels enjoyed some tourist prosperity, English visitors such as anglers were warmly welcomed, got on famously with local people, and are nostalgically remembered as the best holidaymakers of all. The Troubles, although having only an indirect impact on the South, ended that golden era.

'Imbalance of interest' also applies to media coverage. British politics and current affairs are dealt with extensively in the Irish media, both print and electronic, but the reverse is not true, except in 'Irish editions'. And Irish people complain that, while Irish success stories as in sport are labelled 'British', Irish nationality is quickly identified where delinquency is involved.

There is occasional British resentment of Irish success stories, particularly in business, since they are at odds with the 'paddy' stereotype. Given long-standing racist lampooning of the Irish in magazines such as *Punch*, it would be remarkable if residual traces were not to be found today in English tabloids. By the same token, those Tory circles that felt the integrity of the United Kingdom had been violated by Irish secession subsequently resented Irish independence of action in foreign policy. On a happier note, a revitalised Conservative Party leadership in pursuit of electoral success turned to Ireland in early 2006 for economic lessons. More generally, in London cultural and social spheres today, to be Irish is to be fashionable, particularly among actors and comedians. No longer are Irish people seen as guilty by association with the IRA, memory of whose atrocities in England are thankfully fading. Even the anti-Irish joke is out of fashion now.

On our side of the Irish Sea, the main anglophobic voices are to be heard from so-called 'republicans'; not only from unreconstructed dissidents who have a simplistic attitude towards British 'occupation', past and present, but also in a more complex manner, from mainstream Sinn Féin, leadership and rank-and-file. Although they are supposed to have accepted the need for unionist consent to Irish unity, they still rancorously blame the Brits for everything and attribute malign, conspiratorial machinations to faceless British 'securocrats'.

Northern nationalism still lives in the nineteenth century: members of the Sinn Féin leadership are mainly northern, and their sense of the British 'enemy' is strong and recent. In Ireland as a whole, Sinn Féin rejects any part of the British heritage: local activists campaign against the retention of any British relics or monuments (ignoring Santayana's sound maxim that a civilised people does not tear out the pages of its history, but turns them over). This negative attitude is an integral part of their political policies, as well as being an expression of their '800 years of oppression' folklore. Besides, it is good populist politics to throw a soupçon of anglophobia into the stew of social and economic grievances.

In the post-nationalist Republic generally, anglophobia is intermittent and superficial. In 1972, spontaneous nationalist anger after Bloody Sunday led to the burning of the British Embassy in Dublin. By contrast, pro-hunger strike demonstrations in the Republic in 1981 had to be orchestrated by Sinn Féin. IRA violence in the intervening years had dampened Southern nationalist ardour. In 2005, a television documentary on the burning of Cork by Crown forces in 1920 caused a flutter of anti-British sentiment for a few days. Mildly anglophobic ballads are occasionally rendered in Irish pubs and are rousingly chorused. But this is just a pub-crowd convention. A rendition of 'The four green fields' hardly amounts to a serious condemnation of Britain for inflicting partition. It is of interest that singer Ronnie Drew of the Dubliners, on his own recent admission, never sang any nationalist ballad after 1969 that was likely to cause offence. Unfortunately the same could not be said of another singing group of whom it has been observed that they are more 'wolf' than 'tone'.

Those who look for evidence of anglophobia in the Republic might point to the absence of the Union Jack from most flagpole displays, which otherwise include the Stars and Stripes, the EU starred circle, the local or county colours and, of course, the Irish tricolour. Few hoteliers are inclined to explain this curious admission or to concede that it could be seen as offensive to visitors from next door. The late Seán MacBride would see willingness to fly the Union Jack as servile post-colonial anxiety to please. But the opposite is the case: it is the Irish mind liberated from such complexes that is truly mature. But perhaps the most childish and begrudging of Irish habits is that of cheering any team but England when internationals are being televised: the lone viewer who applauds English scores may risk being name-called by one of those unlovely appellations applied by Irish-Irelanders a century ago – 'west Brit' or 'shoneen'[7]. By contrast, England fans find it quite natural to root for their Irish neighbours when their side is not involved. But somehow the anyone-but-England brigade see no incongruity in cheering on their favourite premiership team.

On the other side of this (not-altogether-serious) anglophobic coin, there is a vast spectrum of Irish interest in British popular culture – sport, television soaps, tabloids, magazines, cars, foodstuffs (all vigorously marketed to Irish viewers and readers) and celebrity personalities – not least the British royal family. Even some ardent Irish republicans are secretly avid followers of the minutiae of the trivial lives of the royals. Cultural founding fathers such as Douglas Hyde (author of *The Necessity for De-Anglicising Ireland*, 1892) could not have imagined the further extent of country-wide saturation anglicisation a century later, although they might have been somewhat consoled by continuing popular attachment to some aspects of the native culture – traditional music and Gaelic games, though not, regrettably, the Irish language.

But the most intense, indeed the most bizarre, Irish cross-channel preoccupation is with English football, much to the detriment of the domestic brand, League of Ireland soccer. The games themselves and the individual lifestyles of premiership players and managers get comprehensive coverage in newspapers, and on radio and television. Whether player x will transfer to club y, and for how much, are speculations that exercise the minds of Irish sports commentators almost daily. There is a particular focus on Irish-born footballers playing with English clubs. At weekends, planeloads of Irish fans regularly take off for one or other of the great premiership shrines – Old Trafford, Highbury, Anfield, Stamford Bridge. Arguments rage in the sports correspondence columns of Irish newspapers about the merits or otherwise of specific English teams and individual players. A fan from a remote west-of-Ireland village might lament that 'we' (e.g. Chelsea) didn't appoint a certain manager or purchase a particular player. Such is the extraordinary extent of Irish fan/British club identification.

iv

In the course of growing up (in every sense), I set myself the task of disentangling the enmeshed threads of my inherited 'faith-and-fatherland' fabric. How have I fared, you might ask? In spite of all I've said earlier, the relationship between our two countries has been marked by a residue of historical tensions that I could not wholly escape. Twenty-five years ago I still detected a lingering post-imperial tendency to patronise on the British side. And for all my self-perceived sophistication, I was too willing to display the prickly sensitivity of the scarred ex-colonial. In those early days, passionately espousing the virtues of neutrality as Irish foreign policy, I bristled in argument with Sir David Goodall, that most distinguished public servant and diplomat. I like to think that the warm friendship that subsequently developed between us was symptomatic of the growing closeness between our two countries.

Over the years, I came to realise that loving one's country does not mean hating another one. I evolved from being a nationalist to being a citizen (the counterpart of northern nationalist is southern citizen). My affection for the British part of my heritage came to be politically expressed by me, as an academic and senator, in the promotion of good relations with our cross-channel neighbours. That is why, in the fraught years of the early 1970s, I strove to maintain contacts both with unionists and with British academics. That is why I became, and remain, a regular attender at the meetings of the British–Irish Association (BIA) – of which more anon.

I may say at this point that I have absolutely no objections to the term 'British Isles' as a convenient description (for meteorological purposes, for example) of a geographical grouping, hallowed by long usage. Northern and other Irish nationalists who profess to find the term imperialist and offensive have accused me of mental servility in this respect. The opposite is the case: having post-colonial hang-ups on such a matter indicates the real slave mentality. There is nothing political or proprietary about the expression: after all, the ancient Brits were relatives of ours before those wretched Anglo-Saxons arrived on the scene. Nationalists sometimes have recourse to the 'neutral' circumlocution of 'these islands' – a description, by the way, that makes no sense if used beyond, well, beyond these islands! I once attended a seminar which solemnly debated alternative nomenclatures and, fortunately and predictably, reached no sensible conclusion. On the other hand, I have frequently objected to the unthinkingly patronising habit of some British politicians and commentators of referring to the larger of the two islands as 'the mainland'.

Over the past 20 years, BIA conferences (held in an Oxford or Cambridge college in alternate years) have brought together British and Irish politicians, diplomats, public servants, commentators, journalists and academics, to discuss and analyse the ongoing state of British–Irish affairs, with particular reference to the situation in Northern Ireland. Given the social composition of the participants, it is hardly surprising that the BIA has been disparagingly dismissed as 'toffs against terrorism'. Yet the Association has created and maintained a network of contacts whose contributions to cordial British–Irish relations over the years has been considerable, if in the nature of things difficult to quantify.

I remember on my first visit to a BIA conference, gazing out of the window at the peaceful Cambridgeshire countryside and reflecting on how difficult it must have been for even the best disposed English people to understand the mindsets of Irish neighbours, nationalists and unionists, and to empathise with our bruised and battered experience. After all, England has enjoyed remarkable stability and tranquillity without serious internal conflict for three and a half centuries, or any real invasion for a millennium, the aerial blitz of the Second World War being the only brush with foreign aggression on home soil.

On a lighter and more musical note, I hope I contributed to the education of my English friends by my rendering of Peadar Kearney's satirical ballad *Whack-fol-de-diddle* ('Now, Irishmen, forget the past/ For a happy time is coming fast/ When we will all be civilised/ Neat and clean and well advised/ Oh, won't Mother England be surprised!')

And I now look forward to two important events in the near future, which will further strengthen the bonds and powerfully symbolise a historic rapprochement. One of these is already fixed in the calendar – the visit of the England rugby team to the Gaelic Athletic Association (GAA) superstadium in Croke Park, Dublin on 24 February 2007. There is no date or firm planning for the second event, but it is now only a matter of time: the first state visit of a British monarch to the sovereign Republic of Ireland. And the two happenings will be symbolically connected.

The GAA is a vibrant amateur sporting organisation. Spread in a dense club network across the whole island of Ireland, it has greatly enlivened and enriched generations of otherwise drab lives. Although its basic strength lies in the rural parishes, its intercounty competitions in hurling and Gaelic football are glamorous events that attract impressive crowds. Largely through its own efforts, the GAA has built a showcase superstadium in Dublin at Croke Park (Archbishop Thomas Croke, d. 1902, was the first patron of the Association), which is the envy of other (professional but less efficient) codes such as soccer and rugby – for long regarded by the GAA as 'foreign games'.

Among the founding fathers of the Association in 1884 was the Fenian J. K. Bracken, father of Viscount Brendan Bracken, Churchill's Minister of Information 1941–45; this connection is a remarkable, but not unique, quirk in British–Irish history. The GAA was intensely nationalist – and Catholic – in its ethos, and remained so for generations. It could even have been described as Faith-and-Fatherland at play. But over the past 30 years or so it has had the self-confidence, based on its great popular success, to liberalise itself in a number of respects – successively dissociating itself from political (particularly physical-force) republicanism; lifting the notorious ban on its members playing or even watching 'foreign games'; and ending the exclusion of British security forces and policemen. Now the Association has taken an even more courageous and radical step. It has agreed to allow international rugby and soccer fixtures to be played in Croke Park (accommodation around 85 000), pending the building of a new stadium for these codes.

This momentous decision has been made in the teeth of opposition from a minority that sees the staging of 'foreign games' as a betrayal of the nationalist ideals of the GAA and a desecration of the sacred sod of Croke Park – especially sacred because of the bloodshed on 'Bloody Sunday', 21 November 1920, when Crown forces fired at players and spectators, killing 12 people including a Tipperary player, Michael Hogan, after whom one of the stadium's great stands is named. This small group of GAA zealots are further incensed at the prospect of *God Save the Queen* being rendered in the great citadel of Gaelic games on 24 February 2007, when Ireland hosts England in the six nations rugby championship. However, such dissidents would do well to remember that, in the troubled year of 1973 when Welsh and Scottish 'cousins' declined to travel over to keep their fixtures, it was England, the 'old enemy', that kept its word: 'we may have our weaknesses' said the English captain that evening, 'but at least we turn up'. For that alone, the 2007 England team deserves a warm welcome on what will be a symbolically rich day of rapprochement. And, if Ireland wins, the hurt of centuries will surely be healed!

Once that symbolic hurdle is cleared, and the ghosts of Crown forces exorcised, it will certainly be time for a mature and sovereign Irish republic to receive the embodiment of the Crown as a welcome guest. It is surely anomalous that, alone among our European partners, we have never had a State visit from our next-door neighbour – something I advocated in a Sunday newspaper column many years ago. The historical reasons for the anomaly need not be spelt out but they have now been removed by our recognition, constitutionally endorsed after the Good Friday Agreement in 1998, that the British Crown no longer occupies part of Ireland against our will. Presidents Robinson and McAleese have visited Queen Elizabeth II on terms of great cordiality, and other members of the British royal family, including the Prince of Wales, have been made welcome in the Republic. Obviously, the Government in Dublin would like to see political accommodation firmly and finally working in Northern Ireland before setting in train the arrangements for a fully fledged State visit. And security fears cannot be dismissed out of hand, especially after the unsettling and unexpected Dublin riot of February 2006. But once her anthem is played in Croke Park, can Herself be far behind?

The Visit, with all its historic implications, is only a matter of time. It will be a particularly happy occasion, since the British sovereign will be coming by invitation – and she will be going home again!

Endnotes

[1] In foreign affairs folklore the story is told about Seán T. Ó Ceallaigh (former freedom fighter, President of Ireland 1945–59) receiving the credentials of the first fully fledged British Ambassador after Ireland broke with the Commonwealth in1948–49. Ó Ceallaigh, who was given to occasional whiskey sips to alleviate ceremonial boredom, mischievously referred to 'the historic chains binding my country to yours ...', whereupon a horrified aide whispered a correction, 'links, sir, links!'

[2] A lament.

[3] 'The two weapons of the mind', an Irish-language writer's reference to the virtues of bilingualism.

[4] 'Couple of words', a phrase commonly (and often contemptuously) used to describe minimum lip-service knowledge, or use of the Irish language.

[5] 'Poor old woman', female personification of Ireland.

[6] Loudly lamenting (her sad plight).

[7] An Irish person who is scorned for allegedly apeing English ways and values (seoinín: Seón, variant of Seán or John (Bull) plus the contemptuous diminutive suffix ín).

Bernadette McAliskey

Bernadette Devlin was born in 1947. She was a student at Queen's University Belfast when the Civil Rights Movement started in 1968. She was elected to Westminster in 1969; imprisoned in 1970; gave birth in 1971; married Michael McAliskey in 1973, and in that same year she lost her Westminster seat following a split in the civil rights coalition, which created both the SDLP and the Provisionals. She continued to campaign for the rights of prisoners, self determination and socialism, and opposed the Good Friday Agreement as temporary conflict management rather than conflict resolution. Since her time as an MP in the late 1960s and early 1970s, she has devoted herself to building a successful community infrastructure in her local area of South Tyrone. She has been a keen community activist on a number of subjects, including equal opportunities, women's issues, discrimination and, more recently, racial equality.

Lives Entangled
Bernadette McAliskey

I have absolutely no idea under what pressure and for what reasons Denis Donaldson made a personal choice to become a spy, an active agent of British intelligence. I have no idea why, previously, he made a personal choice to be an active member of the Irish Republican Army. I have no idea why the person who killed him chose to do so, or under whose orders he did so, and in whose interest the self-confessed British agent and suspected double agent was killed.

I could speculate on a range of potential explanations for all these mysteries: everyone else has. But the questions will now never really be answered. The tabloid journalist who, in his paper's words, 'hunted him down' claims to have found him within 3 hours of deciding to look for him. His assassin followed soon after. It would not have been impossible for me to have located Denis and asked him for his account. I wish I had.

Denis was not the first, and may not be the last undercover agent in the service of the Crown in Ireland. He was not the first, and may not be the last to pay for his decision with his life. That we should all know and accept these complexities, without an individual explanation, is a reflection of an inter-island relationship in which lives are entangled rather than entwined.

Some of the simplest things in life are extremely complicated; and some of the most complicated, in the last analysis, very simple. Love, integrity, and whose side you are on are good examples.

Love – rather like 'the totality of relationship between these islands', to quote John Hume's favourite phrase – is frequently marketed as 'lives entwined', either for the purpose of selling Valentine's cards, overpriced roses or diamonds that deny the blood, sweat and tears of their mining, or in order to maintain the legitimacy and moral cohesion that the institution of marriage brings to an established social order. Be that as it may – love is a considerably more complex reality.

Denis Donaldson had a life partner of many years, a daughter, two sons, three grandchildren, sister, brothers, extended family, comrades, colleagues, friends and acquaintances. In varying combinations he was loved, liked, respected by most of these people. Suddenly the Denis people knew, or more correctly, the Denis they had constructed in the totality of their relationship with him, disappeared. The new Denis – British agent, double agent, vulnerable victim or unscrupulous villain and traitor – usurped his identity like some mythical Irish changeling. Every single human being on whom his life had an impact was required to reconstruct his image and their reality. From the public images of him offered up in the media, it looked as if Denis Donaldson was forced by the circumstances of his disclosure to do the same. Perhaps those who killed him could not permit that process to come to its logical conclusion. Denis Donaldson might have told the whole truth to a wider audience than was healthy for 'the peace'. I don't know...

For everyone, this complex and painful disentanglement was informed by many strands in their own lives: personal history and loss; political history; the need for self-protection; fear of guilt by association; the depth of personal or collective betrayal. For some, in its impact on their personal, political or professional progress and ambition, this discovery might have created opportunities. All of this reconfiguring had as its starting point whichever side of the conflict the person was on – their location, so to speak. The potential locations on the map, and the number of persons standing on any one of them, were many.

Yet in its complexity, the map remained simple. They were all, in the last analysis, singularly on their own side. The singular and personal Denis Donaldson they related to no longer existed. The new one did not belong to them. They despised, hated, reviled, even pitied him, in varying degrees; or simply wiped his existence as a person from the horizon of their own world view.

This denial of the intrinsic humanity of a person, whatever his or her deed, is a learned self-defence mechanism. This process of dehumanising the image of the 'other' is how most people on all sides survive the reality of war. New social constructions of Muslims, Iraqis, Iranians or Palestinians as the axes of evil are the latest cases in point.

Only the very brave or philosophical will acknowledge the humanity of their enemy, and their own contribution to the death and destruction around them, whether by word, deed or omission. This does not cancel out their own suffering, their own rights, principles or actions, for which they are willing to be held accountable. This, to my mind, is crucial to the integrity of republicanism as a philosophy.

Gerry Adams referred to Denis Donaldson, formerly a key member of his party, as 'this man'; Gerry Kelly called him 'that man'. People who did not know him at all called him much worse. Colleagues, friends, comrades and brothers-in-arms of the old Denis, many of whom shared his now very public weakness for 'philandering', retreated to some deep overgrown well of Catholic morality to weigh in the balance of political compromise, the moral lessons of adultery. Others dismissed the possibility of so commonplace an activity constituting the source of his vulnerability. Most didn't care. He had crossed the line. He was over. The blame lay with him and with the British, who – it now appeared to the untutored eye – had been spying on themselves until, in the process of doing so, they had brought their own institution down around their ears.

It was left to Martin McGuinness to acknowledge that the two incompatible Denis Donaldsons were the same person, and that before appearing to change sides, this person had contributed significantly to the cause of Irish republicanism and Irish freedom.

It was left to Anthony McIntyre to point out that, as an agent, the role of his erstwhile comrade had been to lure the republican movement down a path of compromise, in which direction McIntyre considered them to have been already stampeding of their own free will and consent, without much need for further intrigue.

There was a much smaller group of people for whom the painful re-evaluation started somewhere else entirely. Particularly in Belfast, in addition to the complex range of emotions shared as part of the republican community, these people had to deal with the reality and implications of their own unique starting point. They already knew that there was only one Denis: and they loved him. That simplicity is extremely complex.

Denis Donaldson, life partner – whose weaknesses could be read like tea leaves by the woman who loved him, lived with him, forgave him his trespasses, supported him in his tribulation, comforted him in his grief, laughed, cried, struggled and survived the trauma of making family life work in the middle of a war – was not loved because of or in spite of what he was. He was loved unconditionally for himself. That didn't make him right, or excusable. It made him loved. Denis as brother, father and grandfather was loved in the same way.

If men understood this much, women's lives would be easier. Even when they were angry, distraught and unable to believe that he could ever be a spy, despite his own testimony to that fact; even when they were quite at a loss to make sense of it all, fearful of its implications, and where it might end – in short, no matter how complicated it became for them, he remained for them essentially the same person. Because he needed them now more than at any other time, they remained unconditionally on his side. He belonged to them still, and they to him.

We each negotiate our singular path through life. Each of us develops his or her unique, multifaceted identity, personal ethics and ideology, and establishes his or her relationships. Each of us has to make choices and decisions, and very few of us can predict accurately the choices we will make when harsh realities conflict with our constructions, and we are caught in the middle.

i

As we all gathered for a quiet funeral service in the family home, already up for sale, it became clear that, beyond the extended family, this was first and foremost a gathering of three generations of women, supporting the living. I watched my daughter protect and comfort her friend in the unimaginable pain of losing her father twice, and later, like a latter-day Mary Poppins-cum-Boadicea, saw her shielding the Donaldson grandchildren with a sunshine-yellow umbrella from the media vultures whose contribution to the process leading up to this funeral was not insignificant. I recalled the death of Airey Neave, and other lives entangled.

This 'defender of little girls with umbrella' had been barely 4 years old at the time. Her own grandad was cutting turf in the moss, and courtesy of a transistor radio owned by a neighbour on the same mission, heard the news. He duly left his spade and came to our house on the edge of the moss to report. The television told the rest, and as he and I hung on every word, he grabbed a quick cup of tea 'in his hand' and returned to his toil. Only when he was well out of earshot, did a very solemn 4-year-old say admonishingly that, 'Granda had not been even one tiny bit sad telling us that about the man who was killed, and the television said he had grandchildren.' Some loyalty to her mother, or precocious wisdom, had afforded me the charity of her silence.

At the time, I think I explained that Airey Neave had made life very hard for all of us, and that sometimes things like war, and what people do to other people, get in the way and make it hard for grown-ups to see things as clearly as children.

War logic dictates the need for spies and agents, as much as soldiers and martyrs. Robin Hill was slightly older than my daughter, or slightly younger, and probably little more than a child himself when he was abducted in Coalisland and shot as an informer. He was also a member of the local soccer club that my husband managed. Most of the furniture in our house came from his father's shop.

Robin was active on the fringes of the republican movement and got picked up by the police, who tried and, it would appear, finally succeeded in recruiting him as an informer. Robin reported this to his comrades and, as the story goes, was encouraged to let the police believe he had been 'turned' and given false information to pass on. All this happened at the bottom of the food chain of handlers and spies, and between them, Robin Hill was destroyed.

On that occasion, I was escorting a European delegation of women on a fact-finding mission across the North. We arrived back in Coalisland late in the evening, and I, with other republicans in the locality, spent most of the night in a futile race against time to try and find news of him. He had been missing for a while and everybody seemed to know the Belfast 'RA had taken him. In the early morning his body was recovered.

An older woman in the visiting group was particularly distressed and traumatised by this. She found herself in a tight-knit village community whose heart was broken and whose loyalties were torn, who sat and argued openly with each other on the rights and wrongs of their attitudes to this death. We listened to her quietly as the thread of entanglement wove another, earlier tale.

In her youth, she had been part of an underground resistance movement against the German Third Reich. Another young woman in the same resistance cell had been suspected of passing information to the Germans, and comrades had been lost. The group, which included my companion and the boyfriend of the accused, tried, convicted and executed the young woman spy and 'disappeared' her body. It was assumed in the village that the Germans had taken her: it was never spoken of again. Now, in this quiet corner, in the middle of this latest consternation, an elderly lady on a peace mission shared her secret with us. Sometimes the only comfort in life is to know that nobody else has had it easy either. The complexity of love, loyalties and identities are not confined to Anglo–Irish relations.

No one who was in Coalisland at that time ever knew the extent or veracity of the accusations against the man who was killed, because we never heard Robin Hill's defence. Nobody in the wider movement questioned these things, because the war existed, and the attrition rate in Tyrone was without mercy. Young Clancy, O'Farrell, Vincent and O'Donnell had all been slaughtered in a carefully orchestrated and planned SAS ambush based on intelligence information from inside the republican family. In the period from 1986 to the ceasefire, 19 volunteers in Tyrone were killed in actions that had been sanctioned by their military leadership. Almost all those actions were compromised when agents/informers provided advance notice to British intelligence.

One of those to die in this series of compromised actions was Jim Lynagh, killed with his comrades by an SAS ambush of an IRA operation at Loughgall. It is currently alleged, by the same media outlet that 'outed' Denis Donaldson in Donegal, that Donaldson was killed in revenge for the death of Jim Lynagh at Loughgall. The media do not explain why those who died with Jim are not included in the revenge equation. Most of those who served with him are also dead.

I knew Jim better than I knew Denis: he was a friend of many years' standing. On 16 January 1981, the Ulster Defence Association (UDA) knocked on my door with a sledgehammer. It was very early in the morning. They arrived in a car which, far from being stolen or commandeered, had been legitimately hired. Documentation relating to the car hire exists, but has never been fully investigated to this day.

What is known is that the loyalist active service unit who left my husband and me for dead were betrayed by British intelligence agents/informers within the ranks of loyalism. They were permitted to enter the house, do their work, and were arrested directly on leaving. There were soldiers lying in the ditch at the door of my house all night. I know this because I spoke with them, as I returned home from a meeting around 1.30 that morning.

My famous last words may well have been 'Have you no homes of your own to go to, instead of lying outside decent people's houses, and spying on them?'

I was fully conscious, but too seriously injured to move from where I lay on the bedroom floor. My would-be-assassin had discharged all his ammunition: the last shot shattered the bone in my leg as I lay on my back, my head almost touching his feet. I have no idea if Mr Watson, who fired that shot, is haunted by it. At a distance of only several feet, perhaps unnerved by the ferocity with which my husband had blocked their entry using nothing but his physical and moral strength, he had fired eight rounds from his nine-millimetre Browning into my body, and after a second's pause that stood between me and eternity, fired again. There was only one shot left. Perhaps he had forgotten that he had also fired at my husband. Had he known it was the last round, I assume he would have fired it at my head. Maybe it was too near his feet. He walked out of my house, in quiet conversation with his two comrades, Mr Grahame, whose job it was to shoot my husband, also left for dead, and Mr Smallwood, who held my two daughters at gunpoint in their beds. My 2-year-old son watched Mr Watson from the bed onto which I had thrown him to avoid him being killed in his mother's arms.

Erroneously, as they left, I assumed these assassins were the soldiers with whom I had spoken some hours before, when I heard a distinctly English voice call out,

'Up against the wall!' I waited for a shot that I believed might kill a neighbour alerted by the shooting into coming onto the scene. A Northern Ireland accent replied, '**** this for a double cross!'

Some time later, a paratrooper entered the house. I assumed he had returned to complete the mission. As he stood with his rifle pointed at my head, and demanded my identity, my potentially famous last words were less repeatable. He explained that the men who had invaded my house had been arrested on leaving. Less than graciously, I enquired why, since he had been lying outside my house, they had not been arrested before entering it. He informed me that his orders were to arrest them coming out. I have no reason to disbelieve him.

I spent some time on a life-support machine. When I recovered, I heard that the home of a unionist politician, Norman Stronge, had been set on fire very shortly after we were shot. Mr Stronge and his son were in the house. They had been shot, and had not survived. Jim Lynagh was blamed for what was described as 'a revenge attack'. I never asked him about it. Too much information in wartime can make life more complicated than you can afford it to be.

But one might now enquire how many deaths British intelligence caused rather than prevented in total, by entwining themselves in the lives of the people of this island.

There are probably at least ten times as many entangled and intertwined lives as there are deaths, injuries, soldiers and camp followers on all sides of this most recent of conflicts between these two islands. Informers and agents, espionage, betrayal and mixed loyalties have been an integral part of the totality of our relationships since giants built causeways and gods took on the clay feet of heroes.

ii

Once more, the dust settles, and whatever passes for normality creeps stealthily in and out of the fading logic of war. People use the empty space in their psyche for other things, until finally everybody acknowledges that, for now at any rate, the war is over.

War, however, is a limited military exercise. The real question that remains is not about the war, which was a consequence, rather than a cause. The real question is left unanswered, temporarily forgotten. It is about equal rights, human rights and fundamental freedoms. It was the campaign for these things that descended into war for many reasons too well rehearsed to deserve space here. Suffice it to say that the primary responsibility for a fair and equitable society in the North lay with the Irish and British governments, both of whom claimed authority over this jurisdiction either by conquest or constitution – neither by peaceful means. Both, from the formation of the Irish Free State, and the amendment of the Government of Ireland Act onwards, abdicated their duty and responsibilities in relation to the people of the North.

It confers no honour on the position of either government that they were finally motivated and mobilised towards negotiating an end to war, not by the relentless death toll, the grinding permanent attrition on either side, the rising prison population, or the passing on of the violence into a second and third generation, but by the rising vote for Sinn Féin. It does little honour to Sinn Féin that they were motivated by the same high principles, namely their belief that the war was preventing their vote from rising even faster. Principles were abandoned on all sides in the pretence that greater motives pertained. Overnight, those who had cautioned against Trojan horses were reconstrued as militarists by the military men of both islands, now carving up between them not the spoils of war, but the potential spoils of peace.

Nonetheless, the peace is made and continues to be tortuously processed. So what progress are we making towards what goals? Against what targets and indicators will that progress be measured?

Shall we take as our benchmark a renewed understanding of the futility of war and violence, and learning to live in peace, in deference to the much-lauded strapline, 'no cause is worth a single life'?

Here we have the spectacle of our neighbouring island, released from the trauma and cost of war in Ireland, turning to fresh wars in Iraq and Afghanistan, and currently contemplating another in Iran. The Republic of Ireland has taken to parading its limited military hardware up and down O'Connell Street like some tin-pot military dictatorship in commemoration of an uprising it has disowned for 40 years. It has shaken the dust off the Proclamation of 1916, which, among other things, summoned the Irish nation to war with its neighbours. Up until very recently, swearing allegiance to this proclamation could land you in the Special Criminal Court in Green Street. Now, apparently, for the Government that abandoned its constitutional right of jurisdiction, it is safe to reclaim the Easter Rising, the Fenian dead, Óglaigh na hÉireann and the mantle of republicanism.

With respect to law and order, Sinn Féin roundly and loudly condemns the looters of vodka, manufacturers of dodgy diesel, suppliers of stolen cigarettes, and those who flog fake jeans, DVDs and cannabis, significant numbers of whom bear an uncanny physical resemblance to members or former members of Óglaigh na hÉireann, to give the IRA its proper title. The UDA and Ulster Volunteer Force have chosen to interpret their inability to secure more than 1% of the ballot box, with or without the bullet, as a form of social exclusion that justifies not only their continuation of hate-based attacks on Catholics, but a whole new line in attacks on black and ethnic minorities and migrant worker communities. There are rumblings in the grey economy on both traditional sides that the only way to keep the Assets Recovery Agency off your back is to toe the political peace-line.

There is, however, more than 10 years after the ceasefire, and almost 10 after the negotiated peace, no power-sharing government as yet, thanks to alleged Sinn Féin espionage – which brings us back to Denis Donaldson, who was arrested as the key figure in that espionage, and who turned out to be a British spy.

Meanwhile, back at the ranch, the 'direct rulers' have made off with our water rates. They are making us pay again, raising our rates, dismantling our hospitals, local government, health boards, education boards; and they won't let us build in the countryside, which is where most of us live. The plain people negotiate the peace as they negotiated the war, and life goes on.

iii

The basic tenets of republicanism, at least in theory, are not based on national identity. They are based on citizenship, and on the rights of individuals to agree collectively the principles and mechanisms through which they will govern themselves. The bottom line of republicanism is the right of every person to make his or her own decision, to take personal responsibility for that decision, and the consequences arising from it.

Modern republicanism originates with Thomas Paine's challenge to the usurpation of the rights of the individual citizen to determine freely, and in free association with his equals, first the principles of self-government, second the mechanism of delegation and accountability to the people, and the people's right to defend their principles, in the last analysis, by the use of arms.

How Paine viewed those entitled to the definition of citizen was limited by his own world view. The rights of women, indigenous peoples in conquered territory, those with a disability, and those without property or land were not in mainstream consideration in a society where God still decided who was born to rule. Paine's arguments were for democracy, accountability and conscience, as against monarchy, authoritarianism and whim. But the context in which these arguments were applied at the time also varied considerably: the new politics created by the Enlightenment was experienced differently by the 'enlightened' in France, America, England and Ireland.

In France the debate and the revolution took place within an established nation state; national identity was not in question. In America it was different. With its king too far-removed, its native population considered barely human, its huge land mass carved up between adventurers, there was little opportunity for a shared national identity. It did not exist. Only in Ireland did the issue of national identity have an impact on the development of republicanism, and vice versa. Whatever independence from Britain was supposed to mean, for better or worse, Hibernia, the Constitutional and the Workers' Republic were inexorably entangled in the same social construction.

Fast-forward another century, and the citizen army, the republican brotherhood and the Irish volunteers, no doubt riddled with agents, spies and informers, raised the stakes and struck out for freedom. The North had already been betrayed, and partition all but agreed. Had everything but partition been conceded, history might have told a different tale. Republicanism might have secured the upper hand. A secular state might have been established to accommodate the different religions. The Constitution might have been spared the ignominy of playing second fiddle to the Catholic Church. The construction, both of our image and our reality, might have been radically different.

In the twenty-first century, as we herald a centenary of partition, the Rising, the War of Independence, and Lloyd George's offer of dominion status, I have a deep sense of foreboding that, should I survive another 20 years, I will live to see a territorially united Ireland within the British Commonwealth. The Irish President will visit England soon – the choice of an area with a sizeable Irish population will acclimatise the English to the waving of tricolours on British soil. The British monarch will visit Dublin, where the reciprocal waving of Union Jacks will break the ice. A mature and stable Southern State will take steps to accommodate the complex realities of the North, and the governments of the day, both North and South, will include Sinn Féin *et aliter*. We will all be reminded that South Africa, role model for all pretend solutions, is a member of the Commonwealth. By that time, this may well be reinforced by the argument that being a member of the Commonwealth has not prevented Australia from becoming a republic.

Recognising and facilitating the totality of relationships and identities on this island, and progressing unification while respecting the British citizens of the North, will all help make the case. The usual choreography of fancy footwork, the soft 'No', the considered response will all follow. Just in time for the centenary of the civil war, Ireland will accept the terms of Lloyd George's treaty. Is this a win–win victory, or the ultimate betrayal?

It all depends whose side you are on, and how you construct the image and reality of the elusive Republic. By that time, of course, we could all be caught up in another world war, in the interests of peace, freedom and democracy and control of the last remaining oil on the planet. For an intelligent species we are remarkably slow learners, are we not?

A wise woman once told me that it took three generations for the wounds and scars of wars to heal, especially if you were on the losing side. Since we have never managed three generations without some degree of war-making between the two islands, this may offer as good an explanation as any for the underlying distrust and antipathy that is masked by good manners among the upper classes, and not masked at all by soccer fans.

Contrary to the construction of my own identity by others, I do not consider myself an Irish nationalist, a Hibernian, nor have I any difficulty with the national identity of others. My deeply ingrained prejudice relates to priests, police, judges and journalists. These powerful professions are constructed as aloof from the tangled mess to which their contribution is significant and persistent. The pen remains mightier than the sword; the book more powerful than the bullet, which probably explains why the pain, death and destruction caused by the misused power of both pen and book is consistently without consequence to the perpetrator.

It all depends on how one constructs the verb 'to inform'.

Liz O'Donnell

Liz O'Donnell is a lawyer, a TD for Dublin South, and the present Chief Whip of the Progressive Democrats. Ms O'Donnell was born in Dublin, educated at Salesian Convent, Limerick, and is an honours graduate of the Law School, Trinity College, Dublin. She is married and has two children. In November 1992 she was elected to Dáil Éireann for the Progressive Democrats, representing Dublin South, and was opposition spokesperson on Health and Social Welfare 1992–93, and Party Whip and Justice spokesperson 1993–97. In July 1997 she was appointed Minister of State at the Department of Foreign Affairs with responsibility for Overseas Development Assistance and Human Rights. She represented the Irish Government at the multi-party talks at Stormont, which culminated in the Good Friday Agreement in 1998, and was promoted to Cabinet as Minister of State to the Government in April 2002.

Not for the faint-hearted: reflections on the Good Friday Agreement, 8 years on
Liz O'Donnell

i

These are the reflections of a practising politician. In many ways, I crossed the bridge from private to public life flying blind. Concerned by the dearth of women in positions of leadership in public life, I had been active in the Women's Political Association for some years, and worked on the presidential campaign of Mary Robinson, my former law lecturer in Trinity. But I had no prior engagement with any political party of any hue. From being a reluctant lawyer, I fell into politics as a result of a chance meeting with Mary Harney in 1991, 4 weeks ahead of local elections.

I had no agenda, apart from being persuaded that I could make a contribution to public life in a party in which there was space for me personally and intellectually. The Progressive Democrats, formed in 1985 by Des O'Malley and Mary Harney, promised to 'break the mould in Irish politics'. The party's credo was one of radical tax reform and prudent management of public finances. It also had a moderate approach to the Northern Ireland issue. Mary Harney had been expelled from Fianna Fáil for voting for the Anglo–Irish Agreement negotiated by Garret FitzGerald in November 1985, an event that provided the catalyst for the formation of the new party.

Desmond O'Malley was more concerned with 'true republican values than with nationalistic myths'. Dismissed by many as an anti-Haughey rump, based more on personalities than principle, the party articulated a new and attractive electoral choice. In his first address as leader, Des O'Malley said[1]: 'I believe there is a great consensus in Ireland which favours a peaceful approach to the problem in Northern Ireland; which favours fundamental tax reform; which favours a clear distinction between Church and State. Irish politics must be transformed. Experience tells me that no such transformation will come from within the existing parties. It must come from outside. There must be a new beginning.'

When I came on board in 1991, the party was in a coalition government with Fianna Fáil, led by Albert Reynolds, a union that came to an abrupt end with the Beef Tribunal[2], following a clash of evidence between the two party leaders. I was one of 10 Teachta Dála (TDs; Dáil Deputies) elected in the 1992 General Election, and served in opposition as whip and justice spokesperson for the party. By 1997 I had just 5 years' high-octane front-bench experience as an opposition TD. With such an inauspicious political pedigree, little did I think that it would fall to me to be one of those charged with negotiating the multi-party talks that led to the Good Friday Agreement.

John Steinbeck's credo that 'a boy becomes a man when there arises a need' (*Flight*, in *The Long Valley*, 1938) was certainly applicable in my case. In June 1997, after taking a hammering in the General Election, my party had been reduced from 10 to four seats. But by a curious cocktail of luck and numbers, a government was formed in which the Progressive Democrats were to play a decisive role. I found myself being appointed as Minister for State at the Department of Foreign Affairs with a key role in Anglo–Irish relations. The next 9 months of my life were to be dominated by Northern Ireland, as the talks intensified across the strands of negotiations.

ii

At that stage there was no peace process to speak of, despite the careful stewardship of the outgoing Rainbow Government headed by John Bruton. The IRA bomb at Canary Wharf and the end of the first ceasefire had seen to that. The new government inherited a moribund situation and depression on all sides.

All that changed when the IRA reinstated its ceasefire on 20 July 1997. The peace process was back on the rails. After a short decontamination period, talks were to kick off in Belfast in September. I spent the summer beefing up on documents related to the peace process and ingesting what was to become its 'glossary of terms'. The Draft Framework Document and Heads of Agreement, and the position papers already put forward, needed to be understood and absorbed. It soon became clear that learning the language of the peace process was a vital ingredient for participation therein. In a political context so devoid of trust and so full of paranoia, loose words could cost lives. I was adamant I was not going to be the one to drop the ball.

The Irish peace process was a government-driven political project, blessed with all-party support in the Dáil. It aimed to find a comprehensive settlement to the Northern Irish question, one that would identify and deal with the causes of the conflict on the island. It was not, therefore, a normal political process but very much a micro-managed exercise in conflict resolution. Very little happened by chance. Yet we had to sustain a line that would not be blown off course by every latest atrocity on the ground, of which there were many. Thanks to desperate efforts over the years to keep the show on the road in the face of constant obstacles to progress, the term 'creative ambiguity' has become synonymous with the peace process in Ireland.

The project was always high-risk for both British and Irish governments. Fundamental democratic principles were at stake. For the sake of peace and an ultimate settlement, should sovereign governments negotiate with terrorists? The state of mind of the republican movement was crucial. Looking back, many of us from the constitutional parties on the island had frequently to suspend our critical faculties about republican *bona fides* and keep our minds on the ultimate prize of lasting peace.

iii

Eight years on from Good Friday – 10 April 1998 – my memories of that final weekend remain remarkably vivid. For those of us who were deeply involved, that day marked the end of a tedious process of meetings, draftings and drama over many, many months. From the outside, it was easy to spot the tension and sense of stand-off. Hopes were high after many false dawns. People were glued to the TV as though they were witnessing a hostage-taking.

Inside dreary Stormont Buildings, fatigue had replaced elation as the hours and days slipped by and merged into one another. Depressed groups huddled together and hung around, grey-faced and apprehensive. We were charged with a life-altering responsibility; few felt up to it. Togged out for our respective parties and government, we were all also there as individuals. We knew that we had to dig deep, to transcend our own tribes in order to find a historic accommodation.

That morning, walking up to Castle Buildings from the boarding-school-type accommodation provided for the Irish delegation's overnight stays, David Andrews and I joked that Tony Blair's 'hand of history on his back' could just as easily turn out to be a boot of history 'up the rear end'. David was anxious and, by his nature, impatient at the prospect of yet more long meetings. Someone with black Ulster humour had coined the phrase 'punishment meetings'. The Taoiseach, pained with the task of finalising these talks on the same weekend as burying his dear mother, was pinched and white-faced. George Mitchell, whose saint-like patience had sustained us through hundreds of fractious bilaterals and plenaries, knew he was going to have to wear the trousers and 'call it' at some point. The tension was suffocating.

Early in the morning it had seemed clear that all the elements of a deal were in place, following days and weeks of intense negotiation. But then the short time necessary for tidying up the texts and preparing final versions started to drag on. We learned of divided counsels in the Ulster Unionist Party; rumours swept the corridors of walkouts, of recriminations, of delay, maybe of rejection. Tony Blair and Bertie Ahern came back in to talk to leaders one last time; Bill Clinton was on the phone. Seven o'clock in the morning became 10, then noon, then four in the afternoon. Early euphoria gave way to exhaustion and then the onset of head-hanging despair; Mo roamed the corridors barefoot and bleary-eyed. I fretted that we might lose control of final texts in the frenzy of last-minute amendments to documents. We nearly lost Trimble on the North/South Bodies[3] list, which was filleted at the last minute.

But finally the word came that George Mitchell, the Chairman of the Talks, was convening a final plenary session. David Trimble had convinced most of his party to come with him, and had agreed to go ahead. Tony Blair had sent him a side letter holding out the promise of decisive action by the British Government if there were not early progress on weapons decommissioning.

I remember the crowds who piled into the humdrum meeting room to witness what we all knew was history in the making – the politicians and officials who had been around throughout being joined by many others, including the cooks from the hard-pressed Stormont kitchens, still in their white uniforms.

George Mitchell was eloquent as ever, but otherwise rhetoric was in short supply. We were talked out. David Trimble, asked if he agreed to the final text of the agreement, simply said, 'Yes'. Everyone else was more positive, save for Gerry Adams, who had to reserve his position ahead of internal party consultations. People forget that the only people who actually signed any document on Good Friday were Bertie Ahern and Tony Blair, with David Andrews and Mo Mowlam, who put their names to the official British–Irish Agreement.

Then it was over. There were tears of exhaustion and hugs of relief. We all spilled out to brief the media amidst the mud and portacabins and freezing wind. The skies opened and drenched John Hume – more than anyone, the intellectual architect of the Agreement – as he gave his press conference.

We flew back to Dublin. Despite it being Good Friday, some celebratory drink was found. The atmosphere was one of unalloyed delight. As one official said, it was as if we were on a team bus having won an All-Ireland or FA Cup final. Arriving home to an empty house (my family had expected me to join them in Donegal for the weekend), I put on the kettle, only to find that there was no milk. The house was cold. I sat in my coat and turned on the television. It was like an out-of-body experience. RTE was still covering Stormont Buildings with endless analysis. The Democratic Unionist Party (DUP) had staged an angry protest, with poisonous exchanges between the loyalist Progressive Unionist Party and Paisley. I didn't share the euphoria. I knew it was only the beginning, and that the scale of change set out in the Agreement was going to be very difficult to deliver.

iv

Eight years on, I still regard that day as a highlight of my contribution to national politics. I do not believe I will ever experience a more awesome period of my career in terms of sheer responsibility. Moreover, I strongly believe that the Good Friday Agreement, and the peace process generally, have been in most ways a great success, bringing about many positive transformations.

Even though the very worst moment of the Troubles, the Omagh bombing, came just 4 months after the Agreement – and I had the grim task of representing the Government at the memorial service for its victims – political violence has effectively now come to an end. It may be a cliché, but like most clichés it is true: hundreds of people are alive today who would not have been, had violence continued even on the scale of the late 1980s and early 1990s. The IRA – belatedly – has decommissioned its weapons and effectively declared that its war is over. I continue to hope that loyalists will follow suit – and bring to an end the murderous conflicts that harm their own communities more than anyone else.

The democratisation that has replaced the conflict, and what passed for politics for so long in Northern Ireland, is still fledgling. Thirty years of tribal conflict has left a legacy of political dysfunction. Politicians are expert in some ways, but one-dimensional. They have no experience of running their own affairs. They remain polarised, and capable only of representing their own tribe.

While Northern Ireland remains economically less vibrant than the South, and excessively dependent on the state sector, unemployment is far lower than historically. Discrimination has been effectively outlawed and the two communities are much more equal than ever before. Belfast and other cities are much livelier and more prosperous. Nationalists, so long driven by a sense of grievance, have a new-found confidence and optimism. If anything, it is Protestants on low incomes or facing unemployment who feel hard done by, their previous ascendancy – as they see it – negotiated away.

A new police service has been created, which is held up as a world leader in terms of accountability and responsiveness to the community. The courts system has been reformed and substantial demilitarisation has now taken place. And while the enduring pain of the victims of violence remains, all eligible paramilitary prisoners have been released.

Economic and social links between North and South are stronger and more mutually beneficial than ever before. One of the great achievements of the Agreement has been to make North–South cooperation to our joint advantage, politically unthreatening to unionists. I recall the total resistance of the unionist parties to discussing cross-border institutions. They saw them as anathema: a Trojan horse in the belly of which lay a united Ireland. One recalls David Andrews's unfortunate description of the purported North South Council as 'not unlike a government', prompting yet another Unionist walkout. Many Unionist figures from the business and other worlds now play an active part in the running of North–South bodies, and in the development of connections generally. Unionists now generally accept that the Irish Government is balanced and fair-minded. No more striking sign of this exists than Dr Paisley's willingness to meet the Taoiseach in Dublin. But it is still early days in that particular courtship.

The relationship between the British and Irish governments, at all levels, is closer, friendlier and more equal than ever before. Great credit goes to Tony Blair and Bertie Ahern, and indeed to their predecessors, notably Garret FitzGerald, John Major and Albert Reynolds. I think that the habit of consultation and partnership is now deeply rooted across the political and administrative systems, and will continue after the Blair/Ahern era – whenever that may be. There are signs, too, that the two governments are willing to press on and insist on a form of power-sharing short of the full Executive.

These are all remarkable and enduring achievements. The Agreement rightly deserves great credit for its central role in bringing them about. It unquestionably marked a profound and positive change in the history of Ireland and of British–Irish relations. That the Agreement was democratically endorsed, North and South, on the same day gives it a status and credibility way beyond a normal political agreement.

V

Nevertheless, it is clear that some fundamental issues remain unresolved. In particular, the relationship between the two communities in Northern Ireland often seems to be no better now than in the darkest days of the Troubles. Indeed, there are those who believe that it may be worse. Sectarianism seems to thrive. There is a limit to what politics can achieve in human relations. Time may well be a more potent force in that regard. One cannot legislate for forgiveness and reconciliation.

Sadly, cross-community, power-sharing institutions – the so-called 'Strand One arrangements' – have functioned only fitfully in the period since the Agreement. They have now been suspended for three and a half years. Despite the best efforts of the two governments to find a basis for their restoration, it is hard to see how this will be achieved. Even if the Assembly and Executive are restored, it remains an open question whether they will, in fact, function as envisaged by the framers of the Agreement – as an example of, and motor for, reconciliation and partnership for mutual understanding. It does not seem as if there is much public interest in, or enthusiasm for, the institutions – hardly surprising given their chequered and unsatisfactory history, but this is depressing nonetheless.

Moreover, despite calls to implement the Agreement notwithstanding the possible absence of the Assembly and Executive, and while there has been much important progress in other areas, these institutions are at the very heart of the Agreement. Without them, there will be no arena within which the leaders of the two communities can work together and determine their own affairs. And while functional North–South cooperation can and should continue to be developed for its own sake, the absence of a Northern equivalent means there is no truly authentic partner for the Irish Government in North–South institutions, even if British Ministers can fill the gap in a practical sense.

At the heart of this dysfunction is an absence of trust among the players. Trust is only starting to build in the context of relationships between the DUP and the rest. The fact is that the deal was done with a different Unionist Leader, David Trimble, whose party was a major victim of post-Agreement politics.

Politically, the main feature of the 8 years since the Agreement has been the weakening and, to an extent, the marginalisation of the political parties that were key to its negotiation and its early functioning – the Social Democratic and Labour Party (SDLP) and the Ulster Unionist Party (UUP) – the so-called 'middle ground'. I also deeply regret the continued erosion of the Alliance Party and, in particular, the effective disappearance from the scene of the brave voices of the Women's Coalition, the Progressive Unionist Party and the United Democratic Party. It appears that only those parties which build up their strength from the extremes inward – the DUP and Sinn Féin – have the political security and authority in their own communities to reach a lasting compromise.

Reaching that compromise would, of course, be immensely important. But at present one has the sense that both parties are quite happy to stay in their own respective comfort zones, rather than challenge themselves or their supporters to reach out and take the further steps needed – whether on devolution or on commitment to policing.

vi

A question I repeatedly ask myself is whether there were aspects of the Agreement itself, or of how it was negotiated, that encouraged or led to the current difficulties. Could these have been changed? And are there lessons for others here?

My overall view is that indeed there were significant flaws in the Agreement and its negotiation. But at the same time, especially in the circumstances at the time, I am not sure these could have been corrected without effectively making negotiations impossible.

From the very start there was an overlap between two rather different processes, with different sets of participants and different issues of concern. First there was the talks process, which in its structure (the three strands of Northern Ireland, North–South and East–West), and in its objective (the negotiation of a new political agreement to transcend the Anglo–Irish Agreement), essentially went back to the Brooke/Mayhew Talks of 1991/92 in which Sinn Féin had not participated, and indeed further back to earlier initiatives.

At the same time there was a peace process, which essentially involved the two governments and Sinn Féin effectively acting on behalf of the republican movement as a whole. This was initially concerned with the ending of violence, and then with dealing with the consequences and legacies of violence, including prisoners, weapons, and the extent of the British military presence in Northern Ireland.

These two processes effectively came together in the negotiations that led to the Good Friday Agreement. The Agreement itself contains sections on all relevant issues. But there was one consistent difficulty that has continued to bedevil its implementation. This stemmed from the fact that progress on political institutions – a matter of interest to all parties – inevitably became tied up with issues, above all decommissioning, over which most parties had little or no influence. In addition, because Sinn Féin had a wider agenda than the other parties – acting as it was, in some cases, as an agent of the IRA – the understandable sense grew among others that the party had a privileged relationship with both governments and was getting special treatment denied to others. This was only exacerbated by the inevitable secrecy in which the peace process had to begin.

A second feature of the process, which was both a strength and a weakness, was the central role played by the two governments. This, again, was inevitable as government policy bore directly on many key issues, not least constitutional change, and the structures and scope of Strand Two and Strand Three cooperation. Moreover the parties, not unreasonably, looked to the governments to act fairly and honourably as cosponsors of the process. But in addition, it fell to the two governments by proxy to drive discussions forward; we urged the parties to engage in discussion with us and with each other, framed the terms of reference for the negotiations, came up with discussion papers, and in the end drafted the great bulk of the Agreement itself. There were some valuable exchanges in the plenary and other sessions of the Talks. The UUP and the SDLP also met bilaterally and, together, thrashed out the details of Strand One. But there was absolutely no engagement between Sinn Féin and the Unionists, and frankly little enough between others.

This meant that the parties had less sense of one another, as individuals and as politicians, than might have been expected, particularly in so small a society. They had not talked through the issues as human beings. They did not understand, much less trust, each other. This was to have major implications for the period ahead, which continue to this day. But, at the same time, without the role of the British and Irish governments – and indeed of the USA – in pushing things forward, it is unlikely that the parties on their own would have taken the lead. The parties became dependent on the governments and seemed incapable of taking the initiative themselves.

Related to this was a lack of public engagement with, or ownership of, the talk's process. Mo Mowlam always bemoaned the fact that it was not a 'people's project'. It was almost exclusively a top-down process, much of which took place in private. The Agreement was negotiated and drafted in sections. Its final shape emerged only very late in the process. Just a month before Good Friday 1998, I remember an opinion poll in the *Belfast Telegraph* which indicated that only 13% of the public expected a deal to be reached. That it did come was an immense surprise. The SDLP's supporters certainly understood, and were primed for the basic elements of, that deal. But it is fair to say that many republicans had not anticipated an outcome that essentially copper-fastened the principle of consent and established a new Assembly at Stormont. Still less had Unionists expected to see a power-sharing Executive in which Sinn Féin would be entitled to sit on the basis of its electoral mandate.

This lack of preparedness had two negative consequences. First of all, it meant that republicans adopted a very cautious approach to the central plank of confidence-building, as evinced by their difficulties in providing a clear commitment to decommissioning. Secondly, and linked to this, many unionists were quite unprepared to make the emotional and psychological adjustments required of them. They seized on the decommissioning issue as a litmus test of republican good faith, undervaluing or discounting the substantial gains registered elsewhere. Soon, republicans adopted the same zero-sum mentality from the diametrically opposite point of view. They eventually moved; but much too late in terms of capturing broad unionist goodwill.

Nor did many unionists internalise the logic underpinning the basic bargain in the Agreement: a recognition on all sides of the legitimacy of Northern Ireland's place in the Union on the basis of the principle of consent, in exchange for action to promote the equality, in a broad sense, of the two communities. Despite the positive constitutional outcome for unionists, they still felt they were negotiating down and losing. Trimble's failure to sell the deal convincingly to his own electorate was disastrous.

Another major flaw was the self-imposed exclusion of the DUP from the deal. This left the UUP fatally exposed, politically and electorally, to DUP rejectionism.

The decommissioning issue also throws into relief the function of language and creative ambiguity in any agreement of this kind. The reality is that the decommissioning section of the Agreement, however clear its objective, was unclear as to where responsibility lay, and even less clear when it came to the consequences of a failure to decommission. Sinn Féin would almost certainly have refused to sign a more clear-cut document. But, with the support of the British Government, the UUP had to act as if the text were more straightforward. It has been suggested by one biographer that David Trimble was aware of the contradictions, but decided to take the risk that progress in implementing the Agreement generally would induce the IRA to move. It turned out that he was right in the long run, but too late for him personally, and for his party.

The Good Friday Agreement has been famously described by Séamus Mallon as 'Sunningdale for slow learners' – meaning the UUP and Sinn Féin. But looking back, it is at least arguable that the Agreement was actually reached too quickly for the parties, and even more so for the people they represent. Possibly a slower and less dramatic process would have given the Agreement deeper roots. The rocky and difficult implementation phase has already lasted more than twice as long as the period between the first IRA ceasefire (August 1994) and the Agreement itself (April 1998). But, against that argument, one has to ask if the passage of time would necessarily have made the issues any easier. In particular, would the republican side have stayed sufficiently committed over a longer course? What if Omagh had happened before, instead of after, the Agreement?

vii

We will never know. But I hope the issues I have raised here will at least prompt reflection on the part of those who seek to manage similar processes. Some of the same kinds of argument – the merits of a top-down versus a bottom-up approach; the desirability of a short timetable; the need for an external actor to spell out the options, even if in harsh terms – are now being rehearsed in the Kosovo final status talks. Similar issues may well arise following the ETA ('Basque Fatherland and Liberty') ceasefire in Spain.

Moreover, much of the discussion of how the international community should respond to Hamas's election victory in the Palestinian Territories has referred to the possible lessons of our peace process and the republican movement's transition from violence to politics. It is essential that certain basic principles be laid down clearly. The international community has done so. The key issues – of non-violence, recognition of Israel, and respect for the commitments the Palestinian Authority has already made – have been set out in straightforward terms. Certainly, the threat or use of violence is incompatible with normal politics. Nor should there be any doubt over the right of Israel to exist in peace and security.

But, at the same time, we need to show the Palestinian people that we respect the democratic mandate they have given to Hamas – this has wider implications for Europe's role and credibility in the Middle East as a whole. And we need to see how a very complex situation evolves over the coming period. Hamas finds itself in an unexpected situation, one that perhaps it did not want to reach so soon. We also have to see how the relationship between Hamas and President Abbas develops.

Clearly, the most immediate issue is the continuation of financial support for the Palestinian Authority. The EU is the Authority's largest single donor. Most of Ireland's own national aid of €4m annually goes to non-governmental organisations or to the United Nations. But there are some issues for us too. The level and organisation of future funding will undoubtedly be linked to political developments. There is an onus on the Palestinian Authority to put its own house in order and to behave constructively in relation to the peace process. At the same time, I do not think it would be right or wise to act precipitately to cause more hardship for the Palestinian people, or to create disruption and instability.

It is also important that we do not lose sight of the big picture. Whatever the difficulties in implementing the road map, its core insights and principles remain valid. Essentially, only a negotiated and mutually satisfactory two-state solution can bring about lasting peace, stability and justice in the region. There are obligations on all parties, including both the Palestinians and the Israelis. I am glad that the clear unacceptability of settlement expansion, and of the route of the separation barrier, has been made clear by the international community.

As regards comparisons between our own peace process and the situation in the Middle East, one has to be careful to avoid simplistic analogies. There are many obvious differences: not least that Sinn Féin started to make significant electoral progress only once it had embarked on the peace process. But I do think there may be some useful general parallels in handling the transition from conflict.

– In our own experience, the most important condition of all is the absence of violence on the ground. Continuing violence makes it very difficult to build trust or maintain dialogue.

– There must be indications that those involved in violence wish to change and want help to move forward. The British and Irish governments both received a clear indication that republicans wanted to embark on a transition process.

– A secure channel for confidential dialogue is a prerequisite. In our process, this role was adopted by a small number of trusted intermediaries.

– While there needs to be clarity about the major objectives of the process under all headings – violence, weapons, constitutional issues – it may be asking too much to expect progress on all these to be made at the same time, or at the same pace. In Ireland, both decommissioning and acceptance of the consent principle were to be achieved in a longer time frame. The notion that 'nothing is agreed until everything is agreed' is a recipe for endless procrastination.

– While it is right to expect clear signals of commitment, it can be counterproductive to demand the use of specific words, or to expect a group to move quickly ahead of its grassroots support base.

– Work needs to be set in a wider political context. The group being asked to change needs to have a sense that movement on its part will be reciprocated. Participants in a peace process must be treated with respect, regardless of their past crimes.

– A permanent secretariat, with a truly independent chairperson from outside, is indispensable. The awesome chairmanship of George Mitchell was a marvel to behold.

– Certainly a lesson we've learned the hard way – one has to have great patience and to be prepared for ups and downs. A peace process is not for the faint-hearted.

In closing

Looking ahead, I am optimistic about British–Irish relations. Building on the historical settling of our differences on Northern Ireland is an exciting prospect. Our new-found economic success has transformed Ireland in so many ways, not least in national self-confidence. And with peace comes an economic dividend.

Burying the hatchet on the vexed quarrel arising from our legacy of colonisation is long overdue. Now that the current and future constitutional position of Northern Ireland is firmly in the hands of the people of Northern Ireland themselves, Ireland and Britain can both move on.

We in the Republic are now free to honour, respect and enjoy aspects of our culture that are British: our built heritage, our literature, and of course our pre-independence history and war dead. While unionists in Northern Ireland are still in the majority, they are a minority on the island of Ireland, and their British allegiance must be respected by a majority that, in any event, is daily becoming more multicultural and diverse through inward migration.

The recent aborted 'Love Ulster' parade in Dublin shows we have some way to go in our tolerance of 'Britishness'. Ireland should be a warm place for unionists. The seemingly endless enquiries into unsolved killings on all sides during the Troubles make closure more difficult. Enquiries into Bloody Sunday, Finucane, Dublin–Monaghan bombings and many more are guaranteed to shed light on murky practices on the part of British governments over the years. This was a dirty war on all sides. We may never have a shared view of history. Certainly, it is far too early for the clear attribution of truth and justice.

Endnotes

[1] *The Irish Times*, 23 December, 1985.

[2] A judicial enquiry, established following allegations in the media and the Dáil of serious irregularities in the Irish meat industry and the complicity of the regulatory authorities. In evidence, Des O'Malley was critical of Albert Reynolds's earlier decisions on export credit insurance. Reynolds, in turn, described O'Malley's evidence as 'dishonest', leading to the collapse of the coalition government.

[3] A wider list of areas for North–South cooperation by way of executive bodies had been put forward by the Irish side; David Trimble insisted the list be reduced.

Ray O'Hanlon

Ray O'Hanlon is a native of Dublin and has lived in the USA for almost 20 years. A graduate of University College Dublin with a degree in politics and economics, O'Hanlon was a reporter for the Irish Press newspaper group before emigrating to the USA in 1987. He is presently Senior Editor of the Irish Echo *newspaper in New York and author of* The New Irish Americans, *a book that explores more recent Irish immigration to America and the political currents that prevailed in the Irish America of the late twentieth century. Married with three children, O'Hanlon lives in Ossining, New York.*

Red, white and blue – and true green too: taking new stock of the American Irish
Ray O'Hanlon

What is Irish America?

The question might appear unusual given the degree to which the term has become familiar in Britain and Ireland, most especially in the past 30 years or so. At one level, Irish America is nothing more than an ethnic identity tag, albeit one raised to new heights of late in a world that is obsessed with listing and categorising people, places, all manner of things.

Calling Irish America a 'community' might be a bit of stretch, because it is a far-flung and varied assortment of people, one that can sometimes be difficult to distinguish clearly from the broader American mosaic. Some Irish Americans are also African Americans. Some have Italian- or distinctly English-sounding names, while others seem to owe ancestral allegiance to the higher-altitude nooks of Scotland.

Irish America, then, is not a homogeneous mass. But those who claim membership have one thing in common: when you ask them where their old-world roots are to be found, they will nod first and foremost in the direction of a small island on the western edge of Europe.

Some – even if they have family ties to other lands – will do far more than simply nod. Irishness, quite simply, is a popular people brand, made more so because this Irish identity blends so very easily with its American cousin. O'Brien, Flanagan and Murphy are American names as much as they are Irish. And there are more holders of these and other originally Irish names to be found in American phone books than on the entire island of Ireland.

Being American then, for millions of US citizens, also means being Irish. On home turf they will describe themselves as being simply 'Irish' in order to distinguish themselves from fellow Americans with differing ancestral ties. And they not infrequently throw out the same appellation when visiting the old, as opposed to mother, country.

This can cause confusion. Many Irish in Ireland have long been inclined to respond to the Irishness claims of their American cousins with puzzlement or indeed comments bordering on the derisive. But such derision is harder to justify in contemporary Ireland, a place that is increasingly taking on the sights, sounds and hues so long familiar to the Irish of the United States.

i

In again asking what precisely is Irish America, one of the first answers that comes to mind has to do with numbers. It is quite simply a lot of people, millions upon millions of them. And if you are looking at them through the lens of a US politician, they constitute bucketfuls of votes. Ignoring Irish America might once have been of little consequence for a bewigged congressman. But the Great Hunger of the 1840s changed that for all time.

As much as it was the end of an old Ireland, the 1845–50 famine was the beginning for modern Irish America: its big bang. And if Tony Blair saw fit a few years ago to issue a British mea culpa for not doing enough to save the inhabitants of that old Ireland, then it can be rightly deduced that Irish America as we know it is, in large part, a British creation.

Less than 30 years after the famine had finally run its deadly course, Ulysses S. Grant, 2 years out of presidential office but contemplating a try at a third term, placed an official seal on what everybody by then had figured out: the bulk of the Irish nation was making its way through life in America. 'I am by birth a citizen of a country where there are more Irishmen, either native born or the descendants of Irishmen, than you have in all Ireland. I have had the honor and pleasure, therefore, of representing more Irishmen and their descendants when in office than the Queen of England does,' Grant told a gathering in Dublin's City Hall during his 5-day Irish visit in January 1879. The 'more' would, over the years, become even more.

Today, visitors to Ellis Island in New York Harbor – the first immigrant to step ashore here was an Irishwoman named Annie Moore – can avail themselves of an informative museum that traces the history of this storied gateway to America, and beyond it the saga that has been the great movement of people to the United States since the birth of the American republic. One part of the museum exhibit is an electronic map of the country. The viewer can enter his or her ethnic ancestry and the map lights up. It shows the distribution of people around the USA sharing the viewer's genealogical background and additionally flashes numbers, totals for different states, and a grand total for the country overall. Pressing the Irish button invariably draws gasps. But a number in excess of 40 million will do that.

In recent years, the number for Irish Americans has been typically rounded up to a precise 44 million. This tally emerged from two US census takes, 1980 and 1990. It should be noted that many in the total could lay claim to multiple ethnic ties. They simply preferred to place Irish at the top of them. The 1990 Census asked Americans to list what they considered to be their primary ancestry. Based on the results, the US Census Bureau, on 18 February 1998, logged in a figure for Irish Americans of 22 721 252, of whom 22 451 511 were born in the USA. The 22.7 million was comprised of people who considered themselves Irish American in a complete sense.

But the census came up with another number under the heading of 'Top 15 Ancestry Groups: 1990'. It spoke of 39 million Irish Americans. These 39 million Irish American souls made up 16% of the US population at the time, and were second in number to the largest ethnic group, German Americans, who came in at 58 million, or 23% of the population. Americans declaring themselves as English-rooted came in third in the table at 33 million, or 13%. The figure of 39 million was made up of Americans who considered themselves primarily and/or partially Irish American. Many of these would have had Scottish roots alongside their Irish lines.

Even so, this new total was still short of 44 million by five million, or roughly the population of the island of Ireland, North and South, in 1990. The Census Bureau listed Irish as an ethnic category, but it also listed 'Scotch–Irish' as an entirely separate category, on top of yet another category designated as solely 'Scottish'. There were, according to the Bureau's tally, 4 334 197 Americans who considered themselves wholly Scotch–Irish. Give or take a few hundred thousand, the summit of the 44 million people mountain was thus attained. The majority of these Americans are a mix of Irish and Scottish descent, and belong to various Protestant denominations.

ii

The first-recorded Irishman on the soil of the future United States bore neither a native Irish nor a Scottish name. His name was Edward Nugent and, like so many on the island of Ireland, he could lay claim to Norman heritage. Nugent was a member of Sir Walter Raleigh's Virginia expedition and, it turned out, a man not to be trifled with. It was Nugent who killed the Indian Chief Pemisapan when fighting erupted between local tribes and the colonists in the early summer of 1586.

The oft-mingling triangle of English, Irish and American, both native and newcomer, would loom larger as the years unfolded. By the dawn of the American Revolution, the Irish, Catholics, Protestants and dissenters had staked their new world claim in significant numbers while spreading themselves throughout the colonies. In due course they would find their allegiances being pulled in diverging directions.

The first St Patrick's Day parades in New York were pieced together by Irish troops serving in the British Army. A few years later, General George Washington was bestowing a St Patrick's Day holiday on Irish soldiers in the Continental Army who were fighting against Redcoats, sometimes in their former regiments.

Not long after the dust of war had settled, Washington's successor as President of the new republic, John Adams, was casting a critical eye in the direction of Ireland and its inhabitants. It was the beginning of what was to become a complex, sometimes perplexing view of Ireland, the Irish and their struggle for independence, on the part of America's chief executives.

Adams, who was rather more Anglophile than Francophone, had secured passage for the Alien and Sedition Acts in 1798. The second president and his Federalist Party were fearful that a combination of rebellious, exiled and truculent United Irishmen, together with Thomas Jefferson's rival Republican Party, might instigate a French-style revolution on American soil.

Jefferson, when he succeeded Adams, took a different tack. In August 1807 Jefferson, now late into his second term, took quill to parchment at his home in Monticello, Virginia and wrote to William James MacNeven, a leader of the United Irishmen who had spent some time in his majesty's dungeons following the failed 1798 rebellion. The letter referred to Jefferson in the third person, as was the third president's habit. MacNeven had previously sent Jefferson a copy of a book he had written, entitled *Pieces of Irish History*. The Jefferson letter was by way of a thank you. The book, wrote Jefferson, was 'a record of documents & facts which interested all the feelings of humanity while they were passing, and stand in dreadful account against the perpetrators. In this the United States may see what would have been their history had they continued under the same masters.' Jefferson, again referring to the United States, revealed to MacNeven how the states of the new nation saw themselves as a refuge from the political storms of the wider world: 'Heaven seems to have provided them as an asylum for the suffering before the extinguishment of all political morality had prepared the scenes now acting in the world,' he wrote.

America's open door to Ireland, closed by Adams, was opened again by Jefferson. MacNeven, who was born in Aughrim, Co. Galway, was one of a number of United Irishmen who ended up sailing to America during the Jeffersonian years. As for the source of Jefferson's Irish sympathies? He might have been listening to the views of his coachman. His name was Joseph Doherty.

iii

Sympathy for Ireland and its plight was a constant, though largely background factor in American politics during the nineteenth century. It began to take visible form in the 1820s with the spread to American soil of Daniel O'Connell's campaign for Catholic emancipation in an Ireland still saddled with the Penal Laws.

But America's sympathy would be tempered by practicality, shunted aside by indifference and, not infrequently, beaten down by outright racial and religious hostility towards Irish immigrants who, by the early years of the century, had started to make their presence felt in Philadelphia, New York, Boston and other cities.

Between 1815 and 1845 more than a million Irish landed in a continent-sized country, the total population of which in 1840 was a little over 17 million. By 1850 it had risen to just over 23 million, in no small part because of the hungry and bedraggled Irish tumbling off ships from Boston to New Orleans. One and a half million Irish made it alive to America's shores between 1845 and 1854.

There were, then, by the outset of the Civil War in 1861, two distinct Irish cultures in the about-to-be sundered United States: the mostly Catholic urban Irish, and the mostly Protestant rural Scots Irish who had blazed trails westward since the Revolution and had populated the Appalachians from Pennsylvania right down into the heart of the deep South.

Irish would slay Irish many times over in the War Between the States. When the war ended in April 1865, it was the urban Catholic Irish who found themselves on the winning side. This stroke of historical fortune would help propel the explosive rise of raw Irish political power in America's cities in the second half of the nineteenth century and the first half of the twentieth. It would lead to a point where the Irish American ward boss, mayor and governor would become a fixture in the nation's political life. It would lead to a moment in time when the legendary mayor of Chicago, Richard J. Daley, could define diversity simply the way he wanted it to be: 'nine Irish guys and a Swede'.

Daley is as good a politician as any to use in raising the point that Irish America was not just millions of vengeful men and women gazing back east to the home island while snarling at English oppressors. Most of its energy and effort was, in fact, turned inward, directed towards the very real, daily task of surviving and thriving in a land and in a system that could be as unforgiving as it was a source of seemingly boundless opportunity.

After surviving and, as was increasingly the case over time, thriving, what energy was left could indeed be directed at other issues, such as religion or self-determination for the wellspring island.

But there were limits. In the immediate aftermath of the Civil War the Fenian Brotherhood, many of its members former Union soldiers, plotted to invade Canada in an attempt to aid their counterparts in the Irish Republican Brotherhood, back across the ocean. The combined efforts of British, Canadian and US forces put an end to a plan that was as naive as it was impossible to execute: seize Canada, or a large portion of it, and hold it hostage to be used in exchange for Irish freedom.

It was the newly elected President Grant who turned the American screw. The Irish had been, and would continue to be, an essential part of American military prowess and tradition, winners, for example, of more Congressional Medals of Honor than any other ethnic group. But the high honours bestowed on the 'Fighting Irish' were only seen as patriotic and positive when such Irish American prowess was focused on defending America – not when it was being directed in an effort to prise Ireland from the clutches of the largest empire the world had ever seen.

The United States had fought a war for union. It well understood the concept. Ireland was not a colony *per se*: rather, in Washington's eyes, it was an integral part of the United Kingdom. What logically, and emotionally, should have been an overwhelmingly sympathetic view in Washington of Irish efforts to repeat 1776 inevitably crumbled in the face of strategic national interest and, not infrequently, the Anglophile leanings of presidents and other powerful figures.

For the agitated and agitating American Irish, this reality would roll on into the twentieth century, and be nurtured by two World Wars, several more localised conflicts and a Cold War during which the 'special relationship' between Washington and London achieved the status of accepted and rarely questioned orthodoxy.

Of course, the mere reality of Anglo Saxon power didn't silence all those Irish American voices, destined as they were to soar again to new heights after partition.

Irish America's unhappiness with the border in Ireland was brought into sharper relief during the Second World War. The Irish Free State was militarily neutral;

Irish America was anything but. However, activist Irish Americans still found it possible to separate the division of Ireland from the global life-and-death struggle being waged on democracy's behalf.

The wartime US Ambassador in Dublin, David Gray, writing to his superiors, duly aired his discomfort:

'There is reason to believe that the subversive American press will be fed from Éire with a formidable anti-partition, anti-British propaganda as the war ends. The beginning is already under way in certain Irish American newspapers. Since no solution of partition is probable in an appreciable future unless Éire should join us in war and give the requisite guarantees for a common postwar defensive system with Britain, only ceaseless agitation, disorder and growing bitterness are in prospect.'

So what was new?

iv

Irish America's future, as it turned out, was rather more diverse. By the time John F. Kennedy was elected president, many big-city Irish were packing their new cars and heading for the suburban version of the American dream. It had taken almost exactly 100 years to move from the very edge to the very centre of American life.

Back across the Atlantic, however, the ghosts of older, harder times were still on the wind. The troubles in Northern Ireland would be, in a sense, Irish America's sole foreign relations issue. But Irish America wasn't a government. How it reacted to the deepening morass in Northern Ireland during the 1970s and 1980s was as varied in tone and appearance as a Noraid fundraiser in a corner bar, and an American Ireland Fund gala dinner at the Waldorf Astoria Hotel. Between the two ends was a spectrum made up of countless strands of opinion and shades of green.

In the end, it all seemed so obvious. Irish American opinion, certainly the great bulk of it, could be woven into one strand around the person of the American President. Of the 41 presidents prior to Bill Clinton, five have held office during the modern Troubles. Two of them, Nixon and Reagan, had easily traceable family lines to Ireland, a graveyard for the former; village for the latter.

It has often been asked what JFK would have done had he occupied the Oval Office when Belfast and Derry erupted. Kennedy's 1000 days were dominated by the Cold War, near-Armageddon during the Cuban Missile Crisis and the early forays into Vietnam. As a US Senator, however, he had co-sponsored a resolution favouring self-determination for the people of Ireland. 'This resolution,' Kennedy later wrote in a letter to a journalist, 'was that the Republic of Ireland should embrace the entire territory of Ireland, unless a clear majority of all the people, in a free plebiscite, declared to the contrary. Unfortunately, our resolution was never passed by the Senate. I hope you will realize, however, that I still favor the idea, and will do everything feasible to advance the cause.'

The resolution Kennedy was referring to dated to 1956. Kennedy's reference to it in the letter was written in 1960, some time between his nomination as the Democratic candidate and election to the presidency.

Kennedy was Bill Clinton's hero and role model. There is an extraordinary photo of the two shaking hands, the 35th president and the future 42nd. What were the odds against such an encounter? No greater than the very idea of an American president pushing Ireland to the forefront of American foreign policy. Tip O'Neill's adage about all politics being local played true when it came to Clinton and Ireland.

New York, of course, is local on a global scale. It was in that city, the borough of the Bronx to be precise, that a group of Irish Americans gathered in 1984 to listen to Walter Mondale and what he might do about Northern Ireland if he knocked the Irish American Ronald Reagan out of the White House. The event was organised by a member of the New York State Assembly, John Dearie, who, like the former vice president, was a Democrat.

By November of that year, Mondale was still the former vice president. But the idea of an Irish American presidential forum had stuck. In 1988, now held in a Manhattan hotel, the forum pulled in the eventual Democratic nominee, Michael Dukakis, along with a rising star in the party, Al Gore.

But it was the 1992 forum that was really to change the course of US involvement in Ireland and, indeed, US relations with Great Britain and Ireland. It, too, booked into a Manhattan hotel, in a meeting room immediately below the bedroom where one of the candidates for the Democratic nomination that year was about to spend a sleepless night. Bill Clinton was ready for any issue that distracted from the Gennifer Flowers mess that had erupted on the eve of the New York primary. He had been persuaded to attend a forum being put together by local Irish American leaders. It had even been moved to his hotel. There was no escape. Besides, Clinton had heard that his chief rival for the party's nomination, former California governor Jerry Brown, was expected to turn up.

Both men did, 4 hours apart on what turned into a Sunday evening–Monday morning marathon. Clinton and Brown said much the same thing in answer to a series of questions posed by a panel. Both were warmly applauded – Brown a little more heartily because the political pundits in the room reckoned he was going to add the Empire State to his earlier primary win in next-door Connecticut. They were wrong. A few days later Clinton came out on top, and from there it was a march of triumph to the Convention and the White House.

Years later, on Air Force One, while returning from his third and final presidential visit to Ireland, a sleepy Clinton would think back to his moment in a room full of expectant Irish Americans, descendants of the earlier huddled Irish masses yearning to be free.

Clinton was, himself, Irish American. He had proclaimed himself as such more than once. 'We had that little meeting,' Clinton told a reporter. 'And I thought, it makes a lot of sense to me. I will do something on this. When the United States is involved, even in a small place, it has big psychological significance. It makes a big difference.'

In this assertion, Clinton had the evidence of recent history in his corner. What was additionally significant was Clinton's reference to the United States, not he himself, his party, or just the person of the President.

The United States, through the years of the Bush presidency, has remained involved in the search for a lasting settlement in Ireland. Its participation has undoubtedly helped pull Dublin and London closer together than has ever been the case since 1922.

But before the United States there was Irish America, sometimes misunderstood, not infrequently maligned and stereotyped, but never for a second forgetful of where it came from, and why.

v

Irish America is now both Democrat and Republican in its political affiliation, a development that should keep Ireland in the policy fold, regardless of which party captures Congress or the White House in the future.

Within the precincts of Irish America, of course, there will be continued argument and debate with Irish America. Was the Good Friday Agreement the end of something, or just the beginning? Will the cessation of violence by the IRA help bring about a united Ireland, or delay it? Can the British be trusted? There's years of debate left in stuff like this.

But the issue of Ireland, its partition, its unity, is on another plane now. This may have been William Jefferson Clinton's doing. It might have been Thomas Jefferson's. It is certainly as a direct result of millions of lives lived, mostly in obscurity, often more in hope than realisation.

If all outstanding issues on the island of Ireland were resolved tomorrow, would Irish America continue to exist? The answer is: yes, it would. Granted, its relationships and dealing with Ireland would shift somewhat. They already have in certain respects, most especially business and economic. But the sense of identifying with a land of origin is a fixed one in the American psyche, even many generations down the path of assimilation.

Irish America has changed the course of history in Ireland and, in more recent years, it has arguably played a significant and growing role in a changing British view of 'the Irish Question.' This is simply a new chapter in a long story. Britain and Ireland together gave birth to Irish America – in all its hues.
At a spring 2006 gathering in New York, hundreds of Irish immigrants

gathered in a church hall to hear Senator John McCain pledge himself to the kind of immigration reform that will secure legal American lives for thousands of Irish who find themselves on the wrong side of US immigration law. McCain, a Republican from Arizona, is a Scots–Irish American, his Irish roots being in County Antrim.

As part of his speech, McCain ran through the story of the Irish in America. He traced a tale of triumph over adversity that was familiar to all in the room. But when it came to the denouement, the halleluiah moment that all present expected to be the salute to John F. Kennedy, McCain reached for another high point in the great Irish American saga. Literally.

He spoke of an Irish American being the first man to put his foot on the surface of the moon. There was momentary confusion. The Irish guy on Apollo 11 was Michael Collins and he piloted the command module when the other two astronauts made their descent to the Sea of Tranquility. Buzz Aldrin wasn't Irish: his ancestral roots lay in Scandinavia. But, of course, McCain was referring to Neil Armstrong, a Scots Irishman by his name.

Nobody cared what precise kind of Irish American Armstrong was. The crowd roared and applauded with approval anyway. On this night in America, the whole world was Irish, the moon too.

Back in 1969, old Mayor Daley was at the peak of his power in Chicago. He ran the city like a fiefdom. Only a year before, he had caused uproar by unleashing his police on anti-war demonstrators gathered for the Democratic National Convention in the Windy City. But on a July night in 1969 Daley, like just about everyone else on the planet, would have been casting his mind skywards to the three men orbiting another world in a glorified tin can. The Irish American political warhorse would have approved of the cosmic trio, the very essence of diversity that they were: two Irish guys and a Swede.

Ruth Dudley Edwards

Born and brought up in Dublin, since graduating from University College Dublin Ruth Dudley Edwards has lived in England, where she has been a further education lecturer, Cambridge postgraduate, marketing executive, civil servant and, finally, freelance writer, journalist and broadcaster. She has been Chairwoman of the British Association for Irish Studies and a committee member of the British Irish Association, the Crime Writers' Association and the Society of Authors. A historian, prize-winning biographer (of, inter alia, Patrick Pearse), and latterly a political commentator, her recent non-fiction includes The Pursuit of Reason: The Economist 1843–1993; True Brits: Inside the Foreign Office; *and* The Faithful Tribe: An Intimate Portrait of the Loyal Institutions. *The targets of her satirical crime novels about the British establishment include the civil service, gentlemen's clubs, Cambridge colleges, the House of Lords, the Church of England, publishing, the Booker Prize and – in* The Anglo-Irish Murders – *the Northern Ireland peace process.*

The Outsider
Ruth Dudley Edwards

I live and work in London; my well watered and often revisited roots are in Dublin, but my childhood memories and my mother's stories of rural Cork are important to me. The political and religious heritage is mixed (Irish Catholic militant republican Grandmother Edwards née McInerney, English Methodist-turned-Quaker Grandfather Edwards, Irish Catholic apolitical Grandmother O'Sullivan née Ford, and Irish Catholic Home Ruler and British Army quartermaster Grandfather O'Sullivan).

It is fair to say that my major intellectual passion is Northern Ireland, where my stamping ground is both urban and rural, centred round Belfast and Omagh. Despite the fact that I was brought up as a (sceptical) Catholic nationalist, since many of my own tribe decided I was a turncoat, almost all my closest friends in Northern Ireland are Protestant and unionist. My long-time crusade has been against the IRA, which has destroyed tens of thousands of lives and made everything worse.

I am best known in Irish nationalist circles for my biography of Patrick Pearse, leader of the 1916 rebellion; in unionist circles for T*he Faithful Tribe: An Intimate Portrait of the Loyal Institutions*; and in English circles for satirical novels making fun of the British Establishment. I am, I think, probably the only person who was, one summer, faced with a choice between a merry shindig in Dublin, a Buckingham Palace Garden Party or observing a stand-off at Drumcree. Cursing, I chose Drumcree.

As everything is copy for me, either as a commentator or a novelist, I think and often feel rather like an outsider everywhere. I have written much that is positive about the political cultures that I aspire to understand, but sometimes frustration gets the better of me. I have endured far too many conferences where nationalists are touchy, unionists are obdurate, neither side tries to understand the other and the English are begging everyone to be rational, believe the best of each other and reach an accommodation – often making use of that maddening phrase of the English political class and commentariat, 'Is the truth not always somewhere in the middle?'

'No, it bloody isn't,' I shout inwardly.

It is not good for one's mental health to spend two or three hours daily reading about British, Irish and Northern Irish politics. The coverage of Northern Ireland in particular can be a source of intense aggravation, not least because so much of it bears little relation to reality. Like politicians, journalists are often so desperate for exciting news that they willingly collude in representing tiny advances as giant leaps and historic breakthroughs, rather than reporting the depressing fact that while Tony Blair and Bertie Ahern may be delighted with each other, nationalists and unionists hate each other just as much as they did yesterday – if not more.

Here, I intend to take the opportunity to reflect biliously on things that drive me mad about various groups on the two islands I love, prompted by a series of quotations from an earlier work of mine identified as capable of further elaboration by the editor of this volume. As a form of catharsis, 7 years ago I wrote *The Anglo-Irish Murders*, a satire on the peace process. The novel is about a conference on Anglo-Irish sensibilities, which has the objective of helping the peoples of this archipelago better to appreciate each other's cultures. This is fraught with terrible difficulties, for, as the English conference organiser rightly points out, all these peoples have been at each other's throats for centuries: 'The Catholic Irish have hated the English and the Protestant Anglo-Irish, certainly, though not necessarily *vice versa*. But the English and the Welsh have always hated each other. The Protestants of Northern Ireland are mostly Scots and hate the English as well as the Irish, and the Scots look down on everyone and since getting their own parliament to swank importantly in, have become as militant as the Micks.'

That analysis seems to me to be so self-evidently true that there is no need for me to comment on it, except to say that there isn't room in this essay for animadversions on the Welsh or the Scots of Scotland.

i

> 'I don't give a shite if we have a United Ireland', he confided, 'as long
> as it has no effect whatsoever on the twenty-six counties.'

A real live Dublin taxi-driver once said that to me, in one sentence summing up
the ambivalence and hypocrisy of southern Irish nationalists towards a United
Ireland. Being prone to enjoying victimhood, they are mostly happy to hang on
to the grievance that the British own Northern Ireland. They vaguely aspire to
acquiring it, and will sing when drunk about the proud old woman who wants her
fourth green field back. They are frightened of the IRA, but many have what is
known as a 'sneaking regard' for the bravery of 'the lads'. Yet in their hearts they
want Northern Ireland only if it doesn't add a penny to their taxes and if there
is a guarantee that those ghastly Northerners stay up there where they belong.

It was not because the citizens of the Republic were self-sacrificing that they
produced a 94.4% vote in favour of amending the constitution to facilitate the
implementation of the Good Friday (as nationalists call it) or Belfast (as unionists
call it) Agreement. The deal involved replacing Articles 2 and 3, which claimed
the Republic owned Northern Ireland; the electorate was keen on the idea
because voting that way made it more likely that Northern Ireland would sort
itself out and they could forget about the bloody place. That they could pretend
that relinquishing the claim was selfless and a cause of deep hurt was a bonus.

The constitution's aspiration to unity was reworded. The new Article 3.1
explains: 'It is the firm will of the Irish Nation, in harmony and friendship, to
unite all the people who share the territory of the island of Ireland, in all the
diversity of their identities and traditions, recognising that a united Ireland
shall be brought about only by peaceful means with the consent of a majority
of the people, democratically expressed, in both jurisdictions in the island.'

Although Ireland sees herself as female (Mother Ireland, *Róisín Dubh, the Shan
Van Vocht, Caitlín Ní Houlihan* – take your pick), from the perspective of Ulster
unionists she is a militant predatory male. There is a lessening of fear since the
would-be bridegroom down south has foresworn the threatened forced marriage
and has, at least in theory, committed himself to courtship. However, since the
majority of people in the south dislike the little they know about their

prospective unionist bride, even as they say they want to wed her, they grumble that she is ugly and rude and explain that they're far too busy for the foreseeable future to take her as much as a bunch of flowers or a box of chocolates.

ii

> 'The difference is,' she shouted, 'that we have a culture and you Protestants don't. Some traditions are not worthy of respect.'

In my novel this is a quote from an Irish-American – a breed it is often hard to love. While most Irish-Americans are Ulster-Scots who take little interest in Ireland, and many of the other tradition are fine people who get on with their lives and don't send money to Ireland for lethal weapons, the militantly republican fringe are a grisly lot of hate-filled, ignorant zealots. I once saw a red-headed, army-booted specimen in the small Fermanagh town of Newtownbutler, where she was assisting fellow republicans to block a legal Orange parade. 'Soon,' she said triumphantly, her eyes shining, 'they won't be able to march anywhere. They should all be sent off to Scotland in a boat.' Even the Sinn Féin councillor she was addressing looked embarrassed.

However, it was not she who first introduced me to that kind of cultural bigotry, but the republican commentator Tim Pat Coogan, who baldly announced 15 or so years ago, at a conference about Northern Ireland, that unionists had no culture. The few unionists present were not inclined to rouse themselves to argue with a well known enemy, but there was panic among English liberals and Irish soft nationalists. 'What about Louis MacNeice?' cried one, only to be contemptuously dismissed by Coogan on the grounds that – like many other Ulster Protestant poets – MacNeice had turned against his own tribe and therefore didn't count.

No one had the wit to point out that, if that was the criterion, Irish nationalists have no right to claim James Joyce, Sean O'Casey and many other writers who fled nationalist Ireland. Indeed, as the nice liberals strained to think of Ulster Protestant composers, ballet dancers or novelists, they showed themselves to be as ignorant as Coogan was bigoted. In the case of the Irish, this was mainly because of both insularity and an underlying conviction that – at best – Ulster Protestants are boring bible-thumpers who are good at do-it-yourself but never had an original idea. As Professor Paul Bew once pointed out when ticking off the normally brilliant Professor Joseph Lee for writing of the 'sterility' of the Ulster Protestant imagination, 'this in the very period when C. S. Lewis, E. R. Dodds, Louis MacNeice and Ernest Walton were flourishing: everything from *Narnia* through brilliant Greek scholarship, outstanding poetry to Nobel prizewinning work in atomic energy.'

This being a largely middle-class group, it occurred to no-one to mention the outward and visible culture of Ulster Protestantism – their bands and parades, which reflect their pride in their origins, and their outstanding musical tradition which, because of its public association with Orangeism, has been successfully rubbished as sectarian drum-thumping. It was clever republican propagandists who – during a period when they were winding up Protestants by stopping them marching – said and wrote that 'Some traditions are not worthy of respect'.

Few people pointed out the paradox. For many years, Sinn Féin has been the most right-on party in Ireland. It makes common cause with minorities, trumpets its anti-racism, multiculturalism and love of diversity, and invites to its annual West Belfast Festival hosts of foreign artists, from the Mugenkyo Taiko Drummers to the Afro-Cuban All Stars, who perform in the time available between cemetery walks and lectures, films and plays about republican suffering and the wickedness of the unionist oppressors. Sinn Féin is a great believer in modish moral relativism: all cultures are good, except that of Ulster Protestantism. In this they are abetted by left-wing Protestants. ('Orangeism is one of those outmoded ideologies of the *petit bourgeoisie* that we must rid ourselves of.')

Of course the Ulster Protestant temperament, its suspicion of intellectuals, its reluctance to boast and its fantastic ineptitude in public relations have a lot to answer for here. Despite the fledgling Irish state's appalling record of banning and driving out its artists, nowadays southern Irish culture is a huge money-spinner and is talked up all round the globe. Homosexuality was illegal until the 1990s, yet the Taoiseach, Bertie Ahern, who is not known as a reading man, opens Wilde's bar and Bosie's Bistro and discourses on Oscar apparently learnedly, while – apart from the intellectual and dethroned leader of unionism,

David Trimble – Ulster Protestant spokesmen are notorious for ignoring their writers and artists and speaking only about one book – the Bible.

While republican paramilitaries inflict mawkish short stories, bad poetry and even the odd dishonest novel upon the world, the contribution of the thugs and half-wits who dominate loyalist paramilitarism has been to shame their whole community by intimidating their fine playwright, Gary Mitchell, out of the working-class estate from which he drew his inspiration. (Republicans hate honesty and criticism just as much as loyalists do, but they intimidate more subtly and with an eye out for the cameras.)

iii

> 'The Northern Catholics never shut up whingeing and the stiff-necked old Ulster Prods, of course, told their side of the story with all the charm and subtlety of an aardvark.'

The first time I was exposed to Northern Catholic whingeing was at university in Dublin in the early 1960s. Having heard from a Belfast girl about the horrors of discrimination, we then learned that she had her fees paid by the British taxpayer and was on a full grant. In the Republic, at that time, there was not even free secondary education, and my gifted working-class boyfriend had to earn his way through university by canning beans in Kent every summer. For him it seemed preferable to be a second-class citizen – as she alleged – in Northern Ireland than a first-class citizen in the Republic.

A few years ago, to show how inclusive they were, the West Belfast Festival invited me – who they regard with deep and justified loathing – to be on a political panel. I tried to explain to the 800 or so Sinn Féin sympathisers that, while it was always tough being a minority, being a minority in the United Kingdom was probably as good as it got. I also mentioned that the Protestant minority in the south had had a rough time, which had been airbrushed out of history. This community – which has been brainwashed with the MOPE (Most Oppressed People Ever) message to such a level of absurdity that they compare themselves with Palestinians and South African blacks – listened politely and then laughed. They had known I was bad. Now they knew I was mad.

But goodness, what brilliant spin merchants and propagandists are Northern Ireland Catholics. Through rhetoric and ruthlessness, republicans, the main perpetrators of violence on the island, have hijacked the human rights industry and convinced most of the world that they are the victims. John Hume – who, from my considerable experience of him, was someone who couldn't stand Protestants – effortlessly projected himself as a man of inclusiveness and ecumenism. David Trimble, who was seen as a bigot, is anything but, and has a group of friends from Catholic nationalist backgrounds who include a retired IRA terrorist.

Trimble saw the need for his people to communicate their message to the world, but he could never do the easy charm or use language he didn't mean. There was a striking contrast when he and Hume made speeches at the Oslo ceremony where they were awarded the Nobel Peace Prize. Hume talked a good deal of familiar high-sounding and optimistic stuff about, for instance, grasping and shaping history 'to show that past grievances and injustices can give way to a new generosity of spirit and action', and ended by quoting Martin Luther King.

Trimble made a thoughtful, realistic and positive speech that drew on Edmund Burke and Amoz Oz and George Kennan (one of the main architects of post-war American foreign policy), and told bleak truths. Remarking that the safest course with such a speech was 'to make a series of vague and visionary statements', he continued:

'Indeed are not vague and visionary statements much the same thing? The tradition from which I come, but by which I am not confined, produced the first vernacular Bible in the language of the common people, and contributed much to the scientific language of the enlightenment. It puts a great price on the precise use of words, and uses them with circumspection, so much so that our passion for precision is often confused with an indifference to idealism. Not so. But I am personally and perhaps culturally conditioned to be sceptical of speeches which are full of sound and fury, idealistic in intention, but impossible of implementation; and I resist the kind of rhetoric which substitutes vapour for vision. Instinctively, I identify with the person who said that when he heard a politician talk of his vision, he recommended him to consult an optician!'

What both communities had to leave behind was the 'dark sludge of historical sectarianism' that both had created, he added:

'But both communities must leave it behind, because both created it. Each thought it had good reason to fear the other. As Namier says, the irrational is not necessarily unreasonable. Ulster unionists, fearful of being isolated on the island, built a solid house, but it was a cold house for Catholics. And northern nationalists, although they had a roof over their heads, seemed to us as if they meant to burn the house down.'

Northern nationalists were outraged at what was represented as a snide attack; republicans greeted the speech as a 'reactionary diatribe'; Tim Pat Coogan said that giving Trimble the prize had been like Caligula making his horse a consul; and a London-based Irish diplomat, echoing the view of the south, told me the whole speech was a disgrace. Northern Ireland Protestants showed few emotions other than deep suspicion.

In due course, prickly, mistrustful Northern Irish Protestants did for Trimble. They also did for the Reverend Brian Kennaway who, with the help of like-minded recruits to his Orange Order education committee, made a valiant and initially successful effort to explain Orangeism to the wider world. In recent years, the Orange Order has suffered from chiefs with the collective imagination of a myopic wood louse and the brains of a flu-stricken hen. Alarmed and paranoid, they dissolved Kennaway's education committee: few even of his enlightened brethren came to his defence.

Lord Macaulay, writing of the seventeenth century, made a brilliant comparison between the Scots and the Irish temperaments:[1]

'In natural courage and intelligence both the nations which now became connected with England ranked high. In perseverance, in self command, in forethought, in all the virtues which conduce to success in life, the Scots have never been surpassed. The Irish, on the other hand, were distinguished by qualities which tend to make men interesting rather than prosperous. They were an ardent and impetuous race, easily moved to tears or to laughter, to fury or to love. Alone among the nations of northern Europe they had the susceptibility, the vivacity, the natural turn for acting and rhetoric, which are indigenous on the shores of the Mediterranean Sea.'

Unfortunately, the Scots who went to Ulster in the seventeenth century – like the Ulster Scots who would go to America in the eighteenth – were planters and pioneers locked in combat with the native population. The hard physical work entailed in working the land left little time for learning other than practical skills, and the siege mentality that developed was inimical to outside influences. (The same siege mentality has often been decried by nationalists, but as a unionist once observed, 'We'd get rid of our siege mentality if they'd lift the fucking siege.')

In the quarter-century that I've been a student of Northern Ireland, I've learned that – contrary to the notion that we will become one happy family when the Protestants see the light and realise that they want to be Irish – we have in Ireland two different tribes, who come from two radically different traditions and who therefore have completely different thinking processes. The roots of unionism, as Trimble pointed out, are in science and the Scottish Enlightenment, which revered reason, discipline and objectivity; the roots of nationalism – dominated by a religion grounded in pre-Enlightenment Scholastic philosophy – are in Romanticism, emotion, subjectivity and mysticism.

I am always amused by the annual shock-horror when a Presbyterian clergymen declines to participate in an ecumenical service. As the present Moderator, the Reverend Harry Uprichard, put it on one such occasion: 'My concern is that the involvement of inter-church worship to that degree publicly aligns those of the reformed faith with those not of the reformed faith.' This is a perfectly logical and consistent intellectual position and has nothing to do with bigotry. From a Catholic perspective, however, although a generation ago it was a mortal sin to go to a Protestant service, emotion now dictates that inclusiveness is all and they will happily pray along with Protestants and, no doubt, Scientologists and Satanists too.

These traditions are reflected in the rhetoric. Ulster Protestants often seem rude and aggressive to Catholics, who they often find insincere and gushing. (To be described by an Ulster Protestant as 'genuine' is a huge compliment.) Not surprisingly, Ulster Protestants often turn out to be nicer, and Catholics less nice, than they seem on the surface. Differences are particularly marked when it comes to the written word, as Trimble again pointed out. Protestants like absolute clarity; Catholics are masters of creative ambiguity. That has led during the peace process to disastrous misunderstandings as well as deepening distrust.

Reason versus emotion are visible too in voting patterns. Ulster Protestants ('I mean proper Prods. Decent unionists who support the state and don't kill people.') do not vote for paramilitaries or their spokesmen. Ulster Catholics do. But Protestants are perfectly prepared to vote for people who come across to the world as raving bigots as long as they are law-abiding, while Catholics will vote for murderers as long as they claim to be peace-loving.

iv

> 'I pay as little attention to Irish politics as is humanly possible. If they are not bombing London, I forget about them.'

I don't blame the English for having become bored and irritable about Irish politics. Essentially, Ireland is a small, attention-seeking country to the west about which English people feel faintly guilty, and which seems forever to be taking offence and demanding a disproportionate amount of money, care, time and apologies. Some of its people are great fun; others are a nightmare.

As an emigrant to Britain from the mid-1960s, I had an old-fashioned and now unfashionable view that, if you aspire to live in someone else's house, you should obey the house rules. Unlike many of my countrymen, I thought it impolite to sing rebel songs about the wicked Brits or to demand special treatment on the grounds that I was of an ethnic minority. Having left Ireland because it was under the authoritarian and misogynistic rule of the Irish Roman Catholic Church, I was deeply grateful to my adopted country for taking me in and treating me extremely well. 'I admire the English for their great hospitality to foreigners and their kindness to strangers', observes one of my characters. My sentiments exactly. This attitude is described in republican circles as 'colonial cringe'.

Not only are the English stunningly tolerant, but they like the Irish very much indeed. Neither in my private nor my professional life did I knowingly encounter any prejudice. Irish victimology is forever harping on about how Irish emigrants in the middle of the last century had to endure signs in English boarding houses saying 'No Irish'. I win no friends by pointing out that your average English landlady wanted a reliable, dull lodger, not someone who was likely to get drunk and bring friends home at dawn. 'If one could only teach the English how to talk, and the Irish how to listen,' observed Wilde, 'society here would be quite civilized.' Certainly – a century later – my English husband and I found that the ideal recipe for a dinner-party was four parts English to two Irish disinhibitors.

There were, however, a few English types who drove me, and still drive me, mad. There were the angst-ridden breast-beaters who revelled in apologising abjectly for all the sins committed by their ancestors in Ireland. 'Ah, but you brought us benefits as well,' one might begin in response, only to be interrupted by earnest assurances that no people in the history of the universe could have behaved worse than the English. I used to snap something about how, if we had to be conquered, I'd rather have been so by the English than the French or the Germans or the Spanish, but that cut no ice with their orgiastic self-abatement.

Then there were the British lefties whose *raison d'être* was to turn every emigrant into a self-pitying burden on the British state. In the 1980s, in particular, shedloads of money cascaded into the begging bowls of Irish emigrant groups and institutions. There was a period, for instance, when left-wing councils poured hundreds of thousands of pounds into appallingly run Irish centres: it took mismanagement on a heroic scale to bankrupt the Irish Centre in Liverpool and to wreck the Irish Club in Belgravia. Yet as these scandals were thrashed out in the Irish emigrant press, their management committees showed no shame: they just demanded more subsidies. This was the period when self-appointed spokesmen for the Irish community were demanding ethnic status, which would give the Irish lots of special privileges and grants, including the right to have a liaison officer in every council, borough or public institution lest the most articulate race on earth might be unable to find the correct words to demand their rights.

Finally, there is the kind of institution that gives grants to notorious grievance-researchers to chronicle discrimination against the Irish. I still remember two complaints in one such preposterous report: the first from an Irish clerk in a social security office who complained that, when Irish people came on the line, her English colleague would suggest she deal with them; the other from an Irish claimant who complained that there was no one Irish in her social security office, so she thought she was probably missing out.

In my early days in London, I led my life almost exclusively among the English, but the bombings and killings made me decide to get involved in matters Irish and do what I could to oppose the IRA. There was the British Irish Association, where I was initially convinced by John Hume's argument that the Irish were a divided people rather than two different tribes. It took me a few years of getting to know players and groundlings on all sides to realise this was rubbish.

Around the same time, I was plunged into the world of Irish emigrant politics when I agreed to be chairman of the British Association for Irish Studies (BAIS) – a new organisation dedicated to bringing authentic culture from all the traditions of Ireland to the British party. What motivated me was the discovery that money was being poured into what can best be described as the Sinn Féin version of history, and there was no organisation to stand up for academic integrity and excellence. I almost choked when I had to listen to a retired lady bomber give a lecture sponsored by Ken Livingstone's Greater London Council in which she said that no people had ever suffered as much as the Irish. The BAIS, which still flourishes, won support from British politicians as well as commercial organisations and did a great deal to take scholarship – including the Irish language – out of politics.

v

> 'The Irish are a very strange people,' said Pooley [an upper-class
> English policeman].

At British–Irish conferences, nice, decent liberals from London and Dublin strain to understand each other's point of view on Ireland, and differences of temperament and thinking are obscured. One of the most illuminating experiences I had in terms of understanding the relationship came at a British–Irish conference that had been deliberately planned so as to exclude the subject of Northern Ireland. 'Let us,' said the organisers, 'model this on Konigswinter, and we will be able to focus on that which unites us rather than that which divides us.' So it was decided that the conference theme should be the European Union.

Yet what was starkly revealed was that the English mindset is Protestant and the Irish is Catholic. As Macaulay said, we are indeed like a Mediterranean nation. At every turn, in looking to the future of the EU, English diplomats urged caution, thinking things through, seeing the implications of arguments, putting brick on brick, and so on and on. 'But surely,' cried the Irish, 'we must have vision. We must think in a European way. We must make a leap. We must remember the Holy Roman Empire.'

I realised that weekend that I no longer thought like an Irish Catholic. Having served my time in the British civil service before it was New Labourised, I had no time for unquantified vision and was preoccupied by the law of unintended consequences. I put on the blurb of one of my books later that I was 'intellectually English and temperamentally Irish'. Inevitably, it caused several Irish people great offence.

However, intellect is not enough. An English failing that, at times, causes me despair is an inability to see evil when staring it in the face. When, in the early 1990s, I wrote *The Pursuit of Reason: The Economist 1843–1993*, I was staggered to find how many brilliant English minds in the 1930s persisted in thinking Hitler was susceptible to reason. When this tendency is in harness with the Irish propensity to wishful thinking, life is good for the bad people. 'The British and Irish governments', says an enraged realist in my novel, 'think that if you invite terrorists to conferences and cocktail parties, they'll give up murder.'

In 1998, David Trimble spoke of his worry 'that there is an appeasing strand in western politics. Sometimes it is a hope that things are not as bad as all that. Sometimes it is a hope that people can be weaned away from terror. What we need is George Kennan's hardheaded advice to the State Department in the 1960s for dealing with the state terrorists of his time, based on his years in Moscow. "Don't act chummy with them; don't assume a community of aims with

them which does not really exist; don't make fatuous gestures of good will.'"
Of course, the British Government ignored him.

As unionists have come to realise, being friends with the Irish Government
is far more important to the British Government than being loyal to unionists.
After all, Ireland is a European and UN partner and, because of her links with
Irish America, can be extremely influential in the USA. When I wrote a book
about the Foreign Office in 1993, I learned about three styles of diplomacy.
Grotian diplomacy was defined by Harold Nicolson as 'common sense and
charity applied to international relations'; Machiavellian diplomats used
'coercion and bribery'; and Kantians sprang from the assumption that mankind
is fundamentally benevolent and will respond to unilateralist gestures of
goodwill. British and Irish diplomats have practised Kantian diplomacy as
republicans played by Machiavellian rules. The mess we have today was
heralded by the catastrophic decision to allow paramilitary prisoners out
of jail without prior decommissioning, which left loyalist and republican areas
under the boot of thugs and criminals. Its most catastrophic legacy is the
destruction of the middle ground of Northern Ireland politics in the anxiety
to appease. In this the Irish and British governments worked hand-in-hand.
Their relationship has never been better. Shame about Northern Ireland.

Endnotes

[1] Macaulay, T. B. (1849) *History of England*, Vol. I, chapter 1, part 4.

Paul Muldoon

Paul Muldoon was born in 1951 in County Armagh, Northern Ireland, and educated in Armagh and at the Queen's University of Belfast. From 1973 to 1986 he worked in Belfast as a radio and television producer for the BBC. Since 1987 he has lived in the USA, where he is now Howard G. B. Clark '21 Professor in the Humanities at Princeton University and Chair of the University Center for the Creative and Performing Arts. Between 1999 and 2004 he was Professor of Poetry at the University of Oxford. Paul Muldoon's main collections of poetry are New Weather *(1973),* Mules *(1977),* Why Brownlee Left *(1980),* Quoof *(1983),* Meeting The British *(1987),* Madoc: A Mystery *(1990),* The Annals of Chile *(1994),* Hay *(1998),* Poems 1968–1998 *(2001),* Moy Sand and Gravel *(2002), and* Horse Latitudes *(2006). He is a fellow of the Royal Society of Literature and the American Academy of Arts and Sciences.*

Rapparee Rap
Paul Muldoon

NOW THAT GERRY MACADAMANT AND MARTIN MACHISMO
HAD BURIED ALL THEIR GADGETS AND GIZMOS
WE THANKED SWEET JESUS THE FAG AND DIESEL SMUGGLERS
HAD TRIUMPHED OVER THE ONE-ARMED STRUGGLERS
BUT WE'D AN UGLY SENSATION THAT LEFT US PRETTY SURE
OUR PIOUS EJACULATIONS MIGHT BE PREMATURE
FOR DEALS WERE BEING CUT WHILE CHRIST HUNG ON THE CROSS
AND THOSE WHO'VE CAST THEIR LOTS COULDN'T GIVE A TOSS
AS THEY TOSS OFF A GLASS OF CHATEAUNEUF-DU-PAPE
IF THE YOUNG IRELANDERS ARE IN LEAGUE WITH THE GOOD OLD CHAPS
AND ALL THE UNDERLYING ISSUES HAVE BEGUN TO OVERLAP
NOW WE'RE DOING THE RAPPAREE RAP

NOW THE RAPPAREES HAVE TAKEN UP DAYLIGHT ROBBERY
AND ALL THE FORMER OUTSIDERS ARE INTO INSIDE JOBBERY
AND THE DISEASE SEEMS LESS ACUTE THAN CHRONIC
WHEN THE SURFACE-TO-AIRS ARE SUPERCHTHONIC
AS CORPORAL PUNISHMENT AND GENERAL DE CHASTELAIN
HAVE LAUNCHED RIGHT INTO AMHRAN NA BHFIANN

AND THE LITTLE BLACK NUMBERS ARE COMING TO THE CRUNCH
AND PADDY'S ALMOST AS PLEASED AS PUNCH
TO KNOW A KIDNEY PUNCH IS A FORM OF BACKSLAP
AND THE CLAPPED-OUT PONY'S NOT HITCHED TO THE CLAPTRAP
AND WE KNOW FINE WELL WE NEEDED THOSE NEW KNEECAPS
NOW WE'RE DOING THE RAPPAREE RAP

NOW THAT GERRY MACADAMANT AND MARTIN MACHISMO
HAVE BURIED ALL THEIR GADGETS AND GIZMOS
AND THE MODERATES MOSDEF NEEDED A DEFANGING
SO AS TO TIP THE SCALES AND LEAVE US HANGING
IN THE BALANCE OF SUSPENDED DEVOLUTION
NOW DE CHASTELAIN HAS GIVEN GENERAL ABSOLUTION

TO THE FILTERERS OF DIESEL AND THE FILTERERS OF FAGS

FOR THE BODY FLUTTERS AS THE SPIRIT FLAGS

WHILE OUR FLAGS AND EMBLEMS ARE STILL IN A FLAP

AND WHAT'S ON THE TABLE IS STILL OFF THE MAP

AND OUR MOST DRASTIC MEASURES ARE STILL STOPGAP

NOW WE'RE DOING THE RAPPAREE RAP